Mobile Devices and the Library

Mobile devices are the 'it' technology, and everyone wants to know how to apply them to their environments. This book brings together the best examples and insights for implementing mobile technology in libraries. Chapters cover a wide variety of the most important tools and procedures from developing applications to marketing and augmented reality. Readers of this volume will get complete and timely knowledge of library applications for handheld devices. The Handheld Librarian conferences have been a centrepiece of learning about how to apply mobile technologies to library services and collections as well as a forum for sharing examples and lessons learned. The conferences have brought our profession forward into the trend and kept us up to date with ongoing advances.

This volume brings together the best from that rich story and presents librarians with the basic information they need to successfully make the case for and implement programs leveraging mobile devices in their libraries. Authors of the diverse practical and well researched pieces originate in all types of libraries and segments of the profession. This wide representation ensures that front line librarians, library administrators, systems staff, even library professors will find this volume perfectly geared for their needs. This book was published as a special issue of *The Reference Librarian*.

Joe Murphy, Yale University Science Libraries, serves as a member of the Handheld Librarian conference committee and leads the field of mobile technologies in libraries as its top speaker.

Mobile Devices and the Library
Handheld Tech, Handheld Reference

Edited by
Joe Murphy

Routledge
Taylor & Francis Group

LONDON AND NEW YORK

First published 2012
by Routledge
2 Park Square, Milton Park, Abingdon, Oxon, OX14 4RN

Simultaneously published in the USA and Canada
by Routledge
711 Third Avenue, New York, NY 10017

Routledge is an imprint of the Taylor & Francis Group, an informa business

First issued in paperback 2013

British Library Cataloguing in Publication Data
A catalogue record for this book is available from the British Library

ISBN13: 978-0-415-68975-5 (hbk)
ISBN13: 978-0-415-84959-3 (pbk)

Typeset in Times New Roman
by Taylor & Francis Books

Disclaimer
The publisher would like to make readers aware that the chapters in this book are referred to as articles as they had been in the special issue. The publisher accepts responsibility for any inconsistencies that may have arisen in the course of preparing this volume for print.

Contents

INTRODUCTION

The Mobile Revolution and *The Handheld Librarian*

JOE MURPHY

Kline Science Library, Yale University, New Haven, CT

The blossoming trend of gearing library services and collections to mobile devices has recently grown from an emerging concept to a high profile and central focus in our profession. The recent Handheld Librarian conferences (http://www.handheldlibrarian.org/) have highlighted and grown out of this shift in focus from the desktop to the handheld as library platform.

This special double issue of *The Reference Librarian* (volume 51, issues 1 and 2), which reproduce talks given at the first two online Handheld Librarian conferences, are dedicated to the work and progress we are making in bringing libraries and their rich resources to our patrons' mobile devices. This focus is about more than technology: it is about a shift in service and possibly even in the roles of librarians and libraries. It is not sufficient to think of this transition as a trend: the statistics cited by the authors within say it all. Mobile usage is neither a fad nor a facet of one demographics' behavior.

The roles of mobile devices in information discovery and engagement are expanding with no end in sight. Librarians exploring this shift now are doing more than reacting to a trend; they are preparing for the future. So let's critically examine this concept together, explore the possibilities, and discuss as a profession how to best adapt to these changes while maintaining the central roles our libraries have always played. The goal of this special issue is to highlight and deepen our discourse around this topic to take this topic from a segmented introduction to a deep analysis.

Here is a brief introduction to the Handheld Librarian conferences by Lori Bell, the primary organizer:

The first Handheld Librarian online conference was held July 2009. The second conference was held in February 2010, and the third in July 2010. Mobile technology in libraries is a very hot topic: everyone wants to know about it and how to implement it in their library. At the same time, travel budgets are being slashed. The mix of the mobile library technology topic and the travel cuts created a wonderful opportunity for Alliance Library System and LearningTimes to provide a rich online conference/training session for librarians all over the world. The topic is changing so quickly which is why it was decided to do this conference twice a year. Each conference has had over 300 registrations with half coming from individuals and the other half from groups which has resulted in 800-1,000 people attending each conference.

Conferences are delivered online via Adobe Connect Pro. Lori Bell and Tom Peters work with a volunteer committee of librarians from all over the US to plan the conference, select speakers, and market the conference. The LearningTimes team provides the Adobe Connect Pro, technical support for attendees and speakers, registration, and the design of the conference website. Alliance Library System was a partner with LearningTimes for the first two conferences. For the July 2010 conference, TAP Information Services and LearningTimes have partnered to produce the conference. (personal communication, email, June 10, 2010)

The Handheld Librarian conferences have continued to grow. A third iteration was held on July 28–29, 2010, and a fourth is planned for February 2011.

In this issue, we will hear from some of the presenters from the first two Handheld Librarian conferences. Their pieces presented here will serve to spark productive discussions as a means of pushing the dialogue on this timely subject forward. Topics covered in this issue range from text messaging to mobile applications, from planning and evaluating mobile services to spotting future trends in mobile technology. A reader of theis special issue can expect a thorough review of mobile technologies and libraries.

We will use the Twitter hashtag #hhlib for this issue to bring this discussion well beyond the pages of this journal and onto our colleagues' cell phone screens around the world in a real time, mobile medium. Include this hashtag when tweeting about this to contribute to the dialogue and search for tweets with the tag to bring together all related posts. Leveraging the Twitter hashtag also helps us bring this discourse into the social and mobile realms, where so much of scholarly communication now takes place.

Whether you are reading this on your iPad, in print, your iPhone, laptop, or Nexus 1, let's use this as jumping off point to move our libraries and our profession forward into and through the adoption of mobile devices.

Launching a Text a Librarian Service: Cornell's Preliminary Experiences

VIRGINIA COLE

Olin Library, Cornell University, Ithaca, NY

BASEEMA B. KRKOSKA

Albert R. Mann Library, Cornell University, Ithaca NY

The Cornell University Library's beta Text a Librarian reference service went live in January 2009. This article discusses the initial six months of the service, touching on the issues of beta testing, implementation, staffing, training, and promotion. It then briefly analyzes the number and type of questions and the development of the best texting practices for reference staff.

INTRODUCTION

Over the past couple of years, cell phones have become more pervasive and the popularity of text messaging has continued to rise. Industry surveys in 2008 indicate that approximately 75 billion text messages were sent in the month of June, an increase of 160% when compared to June 2007 (http://www.cellular-news.com/story/33558.php). Evidence suggests that teenagers, a demographic soon to be entering college, text more frequently than they call (http://www.alliancelibrarysystem.com/trendsreport2009.pdf).

Digital reference services at the Cornell University Library are managed by the Digital Reference Services Committee (Digiref), and both of us are members. Digiref wanted to provide a Text a Librarian service as an additional way for users to reach the library wherever they are, on their preferred device.

IMPLEMENTATION

Research and Development

In August 2008, Mosio approached Digiref to participate as a beta tester for its new "Text a Librarian" software. We decided to partner with Mosio and spent the next few months rigorously testing the software and working with Mosio on features such as protecting patron privacy by not retaining cell phone numbers.

Stealth Launch

In January 2009, we decided to stealth launch a Beta Text a Librarian service at Cornell with minimum publicity. This approach gave us a chance to test both the technology and the user response. We used Cornell University Library (CUL) Labs, a beta launch web site (https://confluence. cornell.edu/display/CULLBS/Home) (Figure 1) to get the word out quietly. During this phase, only DigiRef committee members staffed the service to closely monitor the technology, experience the service first-hand, and learn more about the types of questions and user expectations. During this period, we identified and corrected a few additional bugs and realized that additional features, such as browser sound notifications, were needed. We worked closely with Mosio to improve the software, and signed our first one-year contract in February 2009. Parallel to testing, as we began to get actual user questions, Digiref began to develop new workflows, procedures, staffing models, and best texting practices.

Launch and Publicity

Once we were confident that the software was reliable, we went public with the service and expanded our publicity efforts. In April 2009, we added the option of "Text a Librarian" to our Ask a Librarian home page (http://www.library.cornell.edu/ask) and we began to promote texting through posters, table tents, and business cards (Figure 2).

All of these materials were designed to clearly indicate that a keyword is a required part of the initial question and the limited hours of service. Even so, we frequently received questions after hours. As a result, Mosio provided an after-hours auto-response that directed users to available reference services, such as chat and e-mail.

In the fall of 2009, we trained additional reference staff in texting. The Mosio interface is clean and straightforward, and consequently training on

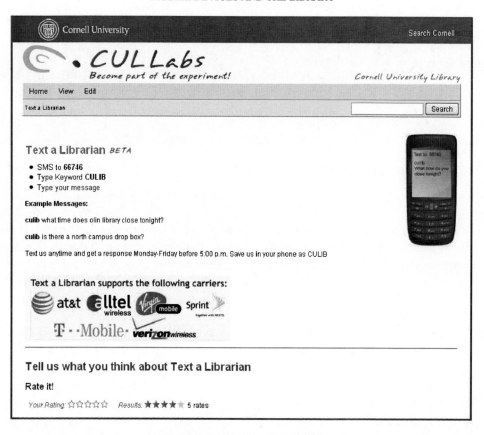

FIGURE 1 Beta launch website.

FIGURE 2 Promotional business card.

the technology was quick and minimal. Acquiring comfort and facility with texting, a new form of communication for most reference staff, is more challenging. The Digiref committee developed a set of "Best Texting Practices" that we used for training and periodically review and adjust. Currently, all staff who provide chat reference are expected to monitor and answer texts.

USE OF THE SERVICE

Numbers and Types of Questions

From April 20 to July 29, 2009, we received 26 text questions. In actuality, we received three times as many questions but these were not real questions; they turned out to be staff testing, practicing, and playing, and these practice/test questions were carefully winnowed out. The remaining number of real questions is disappointingly low, especially since the period included the last three weeks of the semester, a peak period for reference. However, we should bear in mind, that when chat reference services were first established back in 1999 and 2000, numbers were just as low.

At Cornell we offer in-person, phone, e-mail, chat, and now text reference through Ask a librarian. We've avoided providing instructions to users that suggest certain types of questions are appropriate for one mode rather than another. We leave it up to the user to choose, and sometimes we'll move the question to another mode (i.e., from phone to e-mail) for user and staff convenience. Consequently, the types of questions users chose to ask through the initial implementation period of Text a Librarian is quite revealing, as shown by Figure 3.

About half of the questions (14) were quick, concerning hours (4), circulation (2), equipment (6), or a complaint (2), and needed only a brief factual answer. However, approximately half were more substantive questions related to course assignments (6), research or resources (5), or other

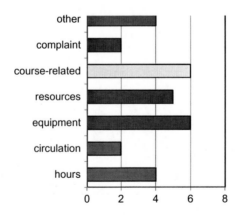

FIGURE 3 Types of Text a Librarian Questions.

(4). The breakdown suggests that, although both librarians and users think texting is a good choice for certain questions, many users are willing to ask complex in-depth questions through text.

Analysis of Interactions

The questions themselves tell us more about user expectations and behaviors. As part of our implementation, we selected and worked with a test population in the spring of 2009. Baseema Krkoska provided bibliographic instruction to an Applied Economics and Management course with 500 students during which she explained the service, encouraged them to try it, and had the students enter the number into their phones. She suggested that they include their Cornell e-mail and course number in their question. Because five of those students followed her instructions about format, they were easily identified in the transcripts. The questions were challenging: "Is philip morris international (PM) ok?" one student asked. Another texted us: "Where would be the best place to find information for a porters five force analysis on a company like nokia?" Obviously several students believed that text was a good method of receiving help with their assignment, even though sometimes staff moved the text question to e-mail where links and more expansive explanations could be provided.

Those of us who offer chat reference will be familiar and not surprised at the fair number of complaints through text. Here is one example: "Is there anyone who reinforces silent study in dean's room? Back of dean's room has become a group study area." Using text to lodge a complaint makes perfect sense—it is quick, easy, and, most importantly, anonymous, because users are often reluctant to be identified when they're pointing the finger. In this case, the complaint also shows that our promotional table tents in the Dean's Room had some impact. Here is another complaint, this time about a resource: "I would like access to the rosetta stone software and know that it's offered to the students in Qatar."

"Can I get some help" one user texted us; it is classified in the "other" category. When we talk with users at orientation events and during instruction sessions, we have become aware that users are intrigued by the Text a Librarian service, but unsure about it—what it is, what it can do, what it is for. Understandably, when most students do not know what reference can do, and when most existing text services are automated—"vote for American idol," "text us for your bank balance." The user who texted us "What sort of questions can I ask? Can I ask if there is a certain book in the system?" is representative of the confusion, a confusion we're trying to mediate through promotion and education.

We are fairly quick in our response times. During the week, staff response is more or less instantaneous or within about 10 minutes. On the weekends, technically the service is not available, but generally staff happens to be monitoring e-mail and see the notification and respond within an hour or two. It is interesting and significant that we get quite a few texts about online resources. Even when users are sitting at a computer, some users prefer to use their cell phone to get help, rather than clicking on the Ask a Librarian web page.

With one or two notable examples, we have not seen a lot of back and forth with users. Users seem to expect a single response which is both challenging and anxiety-provoking for staff who are used to the back and forth of chat reference. On the other hand, many users are quite sophisticated, and load up their questions with lots of precise information so that staff do not have to waste time and text on follow-up questions. "what time is *uris library* open until on may 16th?" (emphasis added.) Our hours are extremely variable and complicated. Note the user giving us specific library and specific date. More examples: "Where can I get a video camera *besides uris?*" (emphasis added.) The most popular place to borrow a video camera is Uris, and the student realized that would be our suggestion. Here, the student realizes access depends on affiliation: "do *cornell students* have access to the Sanborn digital maps database online?" (emphasis added.)

The biggest challenge for staff is the ambiguous question. Again, those of us who offer chat reference are familiar with the initial, unclear question that requires a careful reference interview. In text, like chat, users also seem to be assuming that they're asking quick, factual questions, for instance, "do you have to have a cornell id to take a book out of uris library?" On the surface, the question seems simple, but this was asked during the summer. Was this a current student who'd forgotten their ID card, a graduated senior whose privileges had expired, or a visiting scholar from the area? In our responses, we have been trying to cover as many contingencies as possible.

We used the first six months of questions and our answers to draft a "Best Text Practices" document for staff to follow which incorporates such principles as:

- Adopt a friendly, professional tone.
- Provide clear, concise information-rich answers.
- Don't expect dialogue.

In the future, we plan to continue to learn from text questions and our answers to enhance our best practices and to continue to develop the service based on what we have learned from implementing successful chat and e-mail reference services.

Text Message Reference Service: Five Years Later

BETH STAHR

Southeastern Louisiana University, Hammond, LA

Sims Memorial Library of Southeastern Louisiana University was the first U. S. library to launch a text message reference service. The article describes the rationale, funding, implementation, results, and integration of the service into the Library's suite of branded "Ask A Librarian" reference services. Usage statistics and a breakdown of the types of questions are presented for the five-year history of the service.

INTRODUCTION

Sims Memorial Library (Sims) of Southeastern Louisiana University (hereafter referred to as Southeastern) has always endeavored to be at the forefront of technological innovations in library services. The library and university administrations have supported the initiatives of forward-thinking librarians philosophically and financially. The implementation of a text message reference service in early 2005 is one example of this pioneering character.

Southeastern is a medium-sized public university strategically located midway between New Orleans and the state capital Baton Rouge in the rapidly developing north shore region of Lake Ponchartrain. Although it is primarily an undergraduate institution, Southeastern offers seventeen master's degrees and one doctorate degree. Fall 2009 enrollment was slightly more than 15,000 students. Only 15% of Southeastern's students live in campus housing, and 37% of the students travel more than 30 miles (one way) to campus (Southeastern Louisiana University 2009). Sims is located on the main campus in Hammond, and a branch library is situated at the nursing school campus in Baton Rouge. Two other smaller campus locations function without a library presence.

Cellular telephones are an essential communication tool in twenty-first century America, including our college campuses. A recent Nielsen Report indicated "the average U. S. mobile teen now sends or receives an average of 2,899 text-messages per month compared to 191 calls" (Nielsen 2009, 8). The Student Monitor *Lifestyle and Media Fall 2008 Findings* reported that "nearly nine in ten [undergraduate] students own a cellular telephone" and that text messaging and voice conversation each account for about 37 percent of the time spent by these undergraduates with their cell phones (Student Monitor LLC 2008, 38–9). Similar reports about the ubiquitous nature of cell phone use among teens surfaced as early as 2004, and Sims librarians recognized that this demographic group would have a different preferred approach to libraries than that of our traditional users. With these well-connected "digital natives" in mind, Sims started a text message reference service in early 2005.

Although text messaging was not nearly as prevalent five years ago as it is today, librarians already understood the shift in interpersonal communication away from e-mail to the more mobile and portable Short Message Service (SMS) devices. When Sims' text message service was first implemented, project leaders actually had to seek volunteers among librarians and student assistants to test the software because there were so few "texters" in those early days.

Sims first considered the SMS Reference Service when then Head of Reference J. B. Hill attended the 2004 Virtual Reference Desk Conference and watched a product demonstration by Altarama Information Systems. Hill presented the idea to the library and found support among the reference librarians who were already experienced "virtual librarians." Sims had operated a "chat" reference service beginning in the fall 2002 semester using Library Systems and Services and later Tutor.com software. Sims reference librarians had been encouraged to find innovative methods for reference service and library instruction, so Hill's proposal was accepted with curiosity and interest.

FUNDING

State universities in Louisiana assess all students a Student Technology Fee. The expenditure of these collected monies is restricted and administered by a committee comprised of student and university representatives. Projects are selected for funding based in part on "the number of students impacted by the proposal, the degree of impact on students. . .the degree of reach across various aspects of campus life. . .and the degree to which the proposal advances the University's reputation as a technologically advanced school and being on the 'cutting-edge'" (Southeastern Louisiana University 2009–2011). Hill and Beth Stahr submitted a grant application for a Southeastern Student Technology Fee Small Project Proposal, emphasizing the growing use of mobile telephones, the need for more instantaneous response to library patron questions, and the utility for distance learners who may not be physically able to visit the library for face-to-face reference assistance. A major influence in the approval of the grant proposal was that text message reference services had not yet been implemented in the United States, thereby making Sims the first library in the United States to answer reference questions via SMS. Funding for the service beyond the start-up year came from the library's general budget.

MARKETING CONSIDERATIONS

The service was started in April 2005 using *Reference by SMS* from Altarama. Although some librarians were initially skeptical or wary of the new technology, the team patiently waited for messages to arrive. The messages trickled in, and Sims learned early that this type of service must be marketed consistently and constantly to be successful.

Sims had already established a brand identity for its suite of four reference services. The Ask A Librarian brand represented telephone, e-mail, appointment-based, and online 24/7 "chat" reference. A large, bright green oval graphic on the library web site, bookmarks, posters, and mouse pads provided a familiar reminder of the different ways to obtain assistance from the library. In 2005, the graphic was modified to include the fifth reference service, the new text message service, and its phone number. In 2008, the image (Figure 1) was changed again when Altarama introduced an improved software and local telephone number for Southeastern patrons.

FIGURE 1 Ask a librarian brand from library website.

SOFTWARE SELECTION

The original software, *Reference by SMS*, provided a dedicated telephone number, software to translate text messages to e-mail messages, e-mail messages to text messages, and software to shorten messages into txtspk (also known as textese, chat speak, or text talk). In 2008, Altarama Information Systems (2009) introduced *SMSreference*. *SMSreference* is the same software used by the international InfoQuest text message reference collaboration (Pope et al. 2009, 13). The important enhancements from Sims' point of view were the availability of a local telephone number instead of the international telephone number, which had previously been provided, and the ability to view and answer text message reference questions via web portal, instant messaging, cell phone or other hand-held device, e-mail, or some combination of these. The text message shorthand translator for txtspk was no longer available. However, by 2008 most Sims librarians had mastered the art of texting in their personal lives and were familiar with the shorthand. A significant advantage to the Altarama product was that neither the original software nor the new software required any additional hardware. Installation of the software products was simple and required no ongoing technical expertise.

HOW SIMS USES THE SERVICE

When a text message question is sent to the library's dedicated local telephone number, the software translates the message into an e-mail message. The software works with the campus e-mail system and client. Sims librarians view the converted text message in the same e-mail used for the Ask A Librarian e-mail service (Figure 2). The librarian at the Reference Desk monitors the combined e-mail/text message service and composes answers

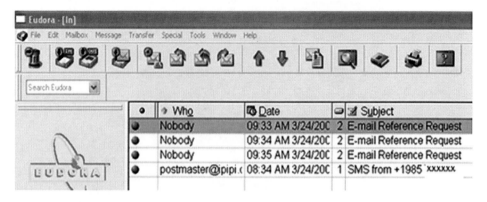

FIGURE 2 Incoming text message question ask a librarian e-mail.

as the messages arrive. Sims library uses Eudora™ for its Ask A Librarian e-mail service, and librarians can easily distinguish between text message questions and e-mail questions because the Sender and Subject displays are recognizable. Patron inquiries and librarian responses that exceed 160 characters automatically generate a second text message. The software translates the e-mail message(s) into a text message and sends the response to the patron's cell phone. The *SMSreference* software also allows the library to check incoming messages from a web portal (Figure 3), an option Sims has not chosen to use on a regular basis. Libraries that prefer to use the web portal will have only incoming text messages and will not have the need to separate SMS reference questions from e-mail questions.

Implementation of Sims' service was easy, and library staff training consisted of a single meeting to review step-by-step instructions. A glossary of textese shorthand and these instructions are available in a binder at the reference desk.

TYPES OF QUESTIONS

Libraries that are considering a text message reference service are always interested in the types of questions that are asked by patrons. There seems to be some concern that this medium would not be suitable for reference transactions. Our questions ranged from directional or library information questions to technology-related questions to real library reference questions. Occasionally, the librarian suggests that the patron call or come into the library for further assistance. Some questions have been unrelated to the library, and the librarian has referred the patron to another campus office. As with any "anonymous" service, Sims received some prank questions. One surprising aspect of the service is that we routinely received "thank you" texts from the patron. This is a phenomenon that was rarely observed in e-mail or "chat" transactions.

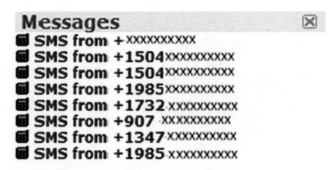

FIGURE 3 Incoming text message question in web portal.

Although the service began operation in April 2005, the archive of incoming questions received via text only extended to July 2006. Based on an analysis of four years of text message reference questions, 86% of the questions were library reference questions, 4% were actually technology questions, 5% were university questions, and 5% were texts which were either inappropriate or silly messages (Figure 4). Few spam messages were received, and Altarama tech support worked with the system administrator to reduce spam.

Patron technology questions included inquiries about the campus wireless system or services at campus computer labs operated by the University Office of Technology. University questions included registration questions, admissions questions, and grade point average calculations. Inappropriate messages included some with a sexual innuendo, but most messages in this category appeared to be silly or prankish (i.e., "What's your favorite color," "What's up," " Im [sic] lost in the library please come find me," "Hello?," and "Happy Mothers [sic] Day.")

Academic librarians are accustomed to answering a combination of simple and complicated reference questions. Text message reference questions varied in complexity and type. Figure 5 shows a breakdown of various reference questions received during the past four years. "LS102 questions" refer to questions about assignments or content from Sims' credit-bearing information literacy course, Library Science 102.

PROMOTING THE SERVICE

Sims began an e-mail reference service in 1997 and the 24/7 chat reference service in 2002. Both services are ingrained in the Library and University culture, and both services are dependent on patron access to the Internet.

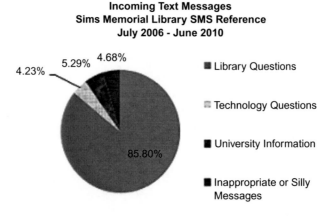

Incoming Text Messages
Sims Memorial Library SMS Reference
July 2006 - June 2010

4.23%   5.29%   4.68%

85.80%

■ Library Questions

▩ Technology Questions

■ University Information

■ Inappropriate or Silly Messages

FIGURE 4 Incoming text message (July 2006–June 2010).

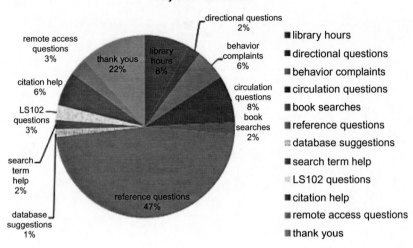

Description of "Reference" Questions
Sims Memorial Library SMS Reference
July 2006 - June 2010

FIGURE 5 Description of "Reference questions" (July 2006-June 2010).

Links on the Library webpage, on the electronic database interfaces, and within the Blackboard learning management system provided easy access to these services. However, originally, text message reference required a different type of marketing, directed at patrons who were away from the Internet and their keyboards. Users needed to be aware of the existence of the service and have access to the correct telephone number. The library's continuing challenge was to find a way to market the SMS service to our students. The telephone number needed to be available to students at the point of need. This type of promotion needed to be sustained and repeated because some portion of the student body changed every year. The service was marketed using the student newspaper, posters distributed around campus, table tents in the library and at campus dining facilities, and on napkin holder inserts in the dining facilities. Librarians promoted the service in more than 200 bibliographic instruction sessions each year and in the information literacy course taken by 1,200 students each year. Marketing strategy needs to progress as technology, media, and usage characteristics evolve. As more patrons use smartphones, which provide access to the Library webpage, the phone number for the service will be available to them. Although marketing will need to be continued, the latest technology innovations that combine Internet access with texting may further enhance this service.

DIGITAL REFERENCE STATISTICS

Statistics on the number of e-mail, chat, and SMS reference questions are available for comparison for the past five years (Figure 6). During this

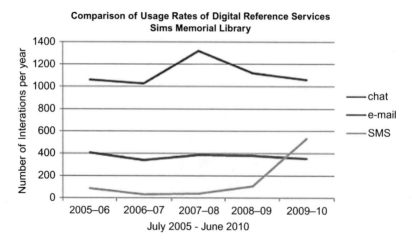

FIGURE 6 Use of digital reference services (July 2005–June 2010).

time, e-mail reference activity has decreased, chat reference transactions have stayed nearly constant, and SMS reference questions have increased dramatically.

The increase in the text questions beginning in early 2009 is explained by the change from the Australian telephone number to a local phone number. Hill, Madarash Hill, and Sherman (2007) identified the international numbers as a challenge because "patrons may be reluctant to send text messages to an international number or may not have cell phone plans that include international text messaging" (27). Furthermore, Sims librarians were reluctant to actively market the Australian telephone number due to these concerns for the library patrons. The local telephone number and proactive marketing beginning in late 2008 account for the increase. For those reasons, it is difficult to extrapolate statistics for the services in future years.

APPROPRIATENESS

Kohl and Keating (2009) described a similar text message reference service at Bryant University as an enhancement rather than a "replacement for face-to-face. . .telephone, e-mail, instant messenger or chat reference" (118). Sims librarians would agree. Although Sims statistics indicated an increase in the use of the SMS service, the overall numbers need to be placed in context. During the 2008–2009 year, Sims' main Reference Desk responded to more than 19,000 face-to-face reference transactions. Kohl and Keating (2009) noted that "text messaging cannot replicate the rich dynamics that an in-person reference interview can provide" (118). The asynchronous nature, the uncertain response rate, the inability to transmit verbal cues like voice inflection, and the 160-character limit are logical deterrents to using SMS for reference assistance. However, digital native media behavior may not be described by logic or a traditional understanding of linking media to need. Sims librarians occasionally suggested that SMS patrons should come into the library or call the library reference desk for assistance with a particular problem. In those instances, the question or research need was simply too complicated to answer via SMS.

In fact, the Library webpage informs students that the SMS "service is good for asking quick, simple questions that can be answered in short responses (160 characters or less). Questions that require lengthier responses should be directed to the Ask A Librarian e-mail reference service. Questions that require immediate answers should be directed to our 24/7 Ask A Librarian Live chat reference service" (Southeastern Louisiana University 2010).

Librarians and information scientists would be wise to consult media user research and media richness theory when considering new media reference services. Media richness theory ranks different types of communication methods along a scale, with face-to-face interactions being rich media and newsletters being lean media. Electronic media (SMS, e-mail messages, and instant messaging) are ranked on a continuum between face-to-face and print media. Daft and Lengel (1986) explained that "the reason for richness differences included the medium's capacity for immediate feedback, the number of cues and channels utilized, personalization, and language variety" (560). Recent management and organizational communication research studies have considered the relationship between media richness and emerging technologies such as SMS and multimedia messaging services (Lee et al. 2007). Froehle (2006) surveyed customers of a large Internet service provider that offered several different media-rich and media-lean customer support services. Library patrons are similar to the respondents in Froehle's customer service satisfaction study, which presented both practical and theoretical implications of new technologies in customer service organizations.

OTHER POSSIBLE USES FOR TEXT MESSAGING

The Sims librarians have identified some additional library uses for this type of service. Broadcast messages could be sent out to students announcing events planned for the library. Book and poetry readings, art exhibits, the Friends of the Library used book sale, library tours, or workshops could be promoted this way. Other library departments can use the software for interlibrary loan or document delivery alerts or overdue reminders, currently being piloted at Sims. Buczynski (2008) included a few suggestions for using broadcast messages including circulation notices, availability of requested materials and library news.

OTHER OPTIONS

In 2004 when our service was first conceived, Altarama was the only vendor offering this type of software. Mosio Text A Librarian now offers similar robust software that should be considered by libraries planning to implement a text message reference service. Another option that has been successful at other libraries is the use of a handheld device (cell phone) to answer text messages. Some libraries opted to use instant messaging for text message reference. Another method for SMS reference was the use of an SMS gateway. Each of these alternatives has advantages and disadvantages, which were discussed in a 2009 review (Stahr 2009). Sims selected an innovative method to work with students in 2004 and has considered emerging solutions over the past five years, but elected to continue with a service that satisfied local needs and complimented the library culture.

USER RESPONSE

Despite some initial concern about whether it was realistic to answer library reference questions in 160 characters or less, Sims reference librarians learned that it was possible to provide assistance and direction with an SMS service. Users' responses have been very positive. Librarians who present bibliographic instruction sessions always explained the five different ways to use Ask A Librarian for assistance, and students in these instruction sessions were frequently surprised and amazed at the SMS service. Instructors who learned about the SMS service in these library instruction classes were generally amused. The combination of telephone, e-mail, online chat, and text message reference provided strong support for the many Southeastern students who commute to the University or who take online classes. Although many of these students do not identify themselves as distance learners, Sims considers these services vital to the academic support of distance learning.

Sims librarians noted that SMS patrons appear very grateful for the service because approximately 10% of the incoming messages during the four years for which statistics are available are thank you messages. Students have been appreciative of the speedy, easy responses that were delivered to them using the medium they selected. Even in those instances where a more robust communication medium was needed to complete the reference transaction, the SMS service was able to provide that important first portal to the librarian.

Text messaging is easy to incorporate into a library reference service. The cost for providing this type of service is low, even when a library chooses to license software to do so. This type of service requires a minimal amount of training or modification of existing reference practices. There are few obstacles to an SMS reference service, and there are good reasons for libraries to offer the service. Libraries that desire to reach a broad set of users will want to add text messaging to their list of reference services.

REFERENCES

Altarama Information Systems. 2009. "SMSreference." Accessed August 18, 2010. http://www.altarama.com/page/SMSreference.aspx.

Buczynski, James A. 2008. "Libraries Begin to Engage Their Menacing Mobile Phone Hordes without Shhhhh!" *Internet Reference Services Quarterly* 13: 261–9.

Daft, Richard L., and Robert H. Lengel. 1986. "Organizational Information Requirements, Media Richness and Structural Design." *Management Science* 32: 554–71.

Froehle, Craig M. 2006. "Service Personnel, Technology, and Their Interaction in Influencing Customer Satisfaction." *Decision Sciences* 37: 1–38.

Hill, J. B., Cherie Madarash Hill, and Dayne Sherman. 2007. "Text Messaging in an Academic Library: Integrating SMS into Digital Reference." *The Reference Librarian* 47: 17–29.

Kohl, Laura, and Maura Keating. 2009. "A Phone of One's Own." *College & Research Libraries News* 70: 104–06, 118.

Lee, Matthew K. O., Christy M. K. Cheung, and Zhaohui Chen. 2007. "Understanding User Acceptance of Multimedia Messaging Services: An Empirical Study." *Journal of the American Society for Information Science and Technology* 58: 2066–77.

Nielsen. 2009. "How Teens Use Media: A Nielsen Report on the Myths and Realities." Accessed August 18, 2010. http://blog.nielsen.com/nielsenwire/reports/nielsen_howteensusemedia_june09.pdf.

Pope, Kitty, Tom Peters, and Lori Bell. 2009. "InfoQuest: Using Text Messaging to Answer Reference Questions." *Library Hi Tech News* 26: 12–3.

Southeastern Louisiana University. 2009. "Electronic Factbook." Accessed August 18, 2010. http://www.selu.edu/admin/ir/factbook/index.html.

Southeastern Louisiana University. 2009–2011. "Student Technology Fee Agreement." Accessed August 18, 2010. http://www.selu.edu/admin/stf/agreement/index.html.

Southeastern Louisiana University. 2010. "Text A Librarian." Accessed August 18, 2010. http://www.selu.edu/library/askref/text/index.html#when.

Stahr, Beth. 2009. "SMS Library Reference Service Options." *Library Hi Tech News* 26: 13–5.

Student Monitor LLC. 2008. "Lifestyle & Media Fall 2008 Findings." Unpublished presentation by Student Monitor, LLC, Ridgewood, NJ.

Will They Come? Get Out the Word about Going Mobile

MAURA KEATING

Douglas and Judith Krupp Library, Bryant University, Smithfield, RI

To be effective, libraries must promote, market, and advertise mobile initiatives. When libraries introduce services that use new tools and modes of thought, they must demonstrate what is possible, how services are relevant, and how new resources can help.

INTRODUCTION

The 1989 movie *Field of Dreams*[1] is often referenced when talking about advertising and all because of one misquoted line. In *Field of Dreams*, Ray Kinsella (Kevin Costner) builds a baseball field in the middle of his cornfield in Iowa after he hears a whisper "If you build it, he will come" and sees a vision of the field. When you are building the first mobile applications for your library users, you might feel a little like this lonely Iowa farmer, doubting your sanity and your ability to fill the stands. Unlike Kinsella, librarians can not rely on ghost baseball players to fill our stadiums. We need to get the word out there. Libraries have been around for a while, but as the world shifts, libraries do too. People are not sure how libraries fit in anymore. If we want to make sure that we stay relevant, then we need to put ourselves out there and that means advertising. Whether you have been using mobile services in your library since the technology first emerged or whether you are just now thinking of implementing mobile services to complement traditional library services, no one will come if they do not know the service exists. Likewise, no one will come if they do not know how to use the service or how the service can benefit them.

In 2007, the staff at Bryant University began to talk about implementing a text reference service at the Douglas and Judith Krupp University Library. After reviewing the options available at that time, including the text reference service Altarama, we decided to keep it simple. Bryant University has a pre-established relationship with Verizon that provided us with an inexpensive cellular phone with a QWERTY keyboard. We chose a plan with the lowest monthly calling minutes possible and approximately 200 text messages per month. Our total expense to implement the texting service was $340. The service now costs approximately $240 per year.

Our staff appreciates the physicality of a phone, as opposed to a virtual service, and it was easy to train everyone on staff how to use it. Most are already comfortable with cell phones. We chose a flip-top phone, the LG enV, to maximize screen space while retaining a physical keyboard. We have since upgraded to an Android smartphone, the Motorola Droid, and again chose to keep a physical keyboard. A service such as Google Voice, formerly Grand Central, is another way to add short message service (SMS) to a library's list of offered services. Google Voice enables users to send free SMS messages using a computer. If you use a phone, standard messaging rates for your service still apply. Google Voice is quick, cost-effective, and easy—now that an invite is no longer required.

At Bryant University Library, we currently use a cell phone service, complemented with Google Voice. Google Voice calls can be forwarded to our other line and to e-mail addresses to ensure that we do not miss a message. At this time, we use Google Voice primarily to initiate texts. It is the perfect tool to copy and paste call numbers from the library catalog to send to patrons. Bryant is also experimenting with augmenting our Google Voice service with GVMax, a free web service that can send Google Voice notifications via Instant Messenger, e-mail, SMS, and more. Since we use Meebo for our Chat reference, GVMax could push incoming SMS messages to the Meebo client, making it even easier for our librarians to respond to a text reference question.

Google Voice features a widget that enables visitors to a web page to call a Google Voice number without dialing. The widget is interesting, but a widget with alternative functionality would be better for libraries. In our academic library, phone calls from our patrons are rare, unless they are calling to see whether we are open. Instead of a phone call, I wish that there were a Google Voice widget that would enable visitors on a web page to send a text message. Ideally, the widget would allow a user to enter a cell phone number with SMS service. Responses from the librarian would be forwarded to the user's text messaging service. The users would be able to take the conversation with them and the library's Google Voice telephone number would remain in the user's call history once a librarian responded.

It would make it that much easier for the user to save the library's telephone number for future reference queries. Widgets, such as the one imagined above or the Meebo widget popular at many libraries, are not only useful, they also serve to advertise a library's services to compensate for the valuable screen real estate that they inhabit on a web page.

In addition to widgets, there are other ways to advertise online without spending a penny:

- Your web site (of course): Advertise and promote the variety of services available at your library on your home page and any other pages relevant to the services in question.
- Social media: blogs (internal and external), Twitter, Facebook, or Foursquare. The landscape of social media is a constant ebb and flow. Pay attention to your users—where are they pointing their mobile devices? You should be there too.

Of course, we advertise offline too. You can find information about us, how to contact us, and what we do in the following ways:

- Paper: We put a simple box with our contact information on the bottom of handouts, pathfinders, brochures, and notepads. The notepads are made by hand by the Copy Center at Bryant University using new or recycled computer paper. We use them whenever we need to write something down for people to ensure that they can contact us again quickly and easily.
- E-mail signatures.
- Library newsletter: Our newsletter is circulated by e-mail to the entire campus. Paper copies in color are delivered to some offices and are on display in the library at public desks.
- Cards (traditional business cards and Moo MiniCards): All Bryant library employees carry traditional business cards. Part-time employees have generic cards where they can write their name. Although the Bryant business cards are standard issue, our clientele are not. We added a standard Avery label sticker on the back of our business cards to customize them and highlight the services that we want to promote and those that our clientele think are important. Our students are much more likely to use instant messaging (IM) than our fax number (and many of our colleagues too). Moo MiniCards are small cards, about half the size of a traditional business card, with a photo or design on one side and text on the other. You can customize Moo MiniCards with your own design or use Moo's ready-made designs. The Moo MiniCards are yet another way to expand advertising—students think they look "cool" and they attract attention. Because each design can be different, Moo MiniCards look colorful and fun spread out on a public desk or on tables when we are roving, like a

rainbow. If you punch a small hole in the end of a Moo MiniCard, you can add them to a keychain with a small ring or transform them into a bookmark by adding a tassel.

- AxisTV Signage: flat-screen televisions scattered throughout campus provide dynamic, "just in time" advertising. AxisTV's digital signs can be programmed to display bulletins, tickers, audio, and video. Creating new content is as easy as making a new Powerpoint slide. At Bryant, we currently have 13 screens, plus one cable TV channel, displaying AxisTV content. Each screen is fed from five different players and each player serves up unique content. For example, the library has its own player and we have two screens—one next to the reference desk and one by the front door of the library. AxisTV is easily recreated on a smaller scale—just run a Powerpoint presentation on an old computer. There are also many free software applications that can display RSS or Twitter feeds as a screen saver.

- QR Codes: the library has begun to use QR (Quick Response) Codes or 2D barcodes as a way to enable users to quickly access our web pages using their mobile phones. We display codes on AxisTV and in paper advertising. We have tied the codes into our "Ask a Librarian" campaign as a way to educate our users about how to use QR codes.

- Tear-off Flyers: we added tear-off slips at the bottom of paper advertisements with the "Text a Librarian" telephone number. We post these simple and popular advertisements on bulletin boards and in rest rooms across campus.

- Informal advertising: we publicize services through library tours, those given internally by our staff as well as external tours given by the Admissions department. Every year, a librarian trains the tour guides on campus. It is a great opportunity to reach incoming students and parents, as well as the tour guides themselves. We advertise our services during information literacy instruction sessions, especially to the "Foundations for Learning" classes, a first-year experience class. Many first-year students will not be doing research at the time of their first interaction with a librarian. Although the details about how to do research may fade from their inundated brains, we want them to remember the services that we offer, that reference librarians are friendly, and that we will be there to help them when they do need us.

- Promotions: from time to time, when special events or a surplus in the budget allow, we invest in promotional items, such as pens, magnets, decals, or even can coolers. These promotional items serve as reminders or visual cues and are usually designed for a particular target market, from students to potential library donors.

From our home page to the ladies' room, we try to think about advertising everywhere our patrons are. One student told me, "Most students don't know what clubs are on campus, but everyone knows that they can text a librarian."

They say that the first impression is everything. Advertisements begin as an introduction, the prelude to a potential relationship. The service that users actually receive at the library is the real test. Did the service meet a user's expectations? Was the outcome what the user needed? Once a user has had an opportunity to try the services available at a library, advertisements become a reminder. It is hard for people to abandon what they know, what they are familiar with, and what is habit. Google is easy, and many students may be more comfortable asking Mom. As librarians, we need to get them out of that rut. An advertisement may help to jumpstart their memory to recall how easy text services can be and how a librarian may help.

Companies such as Cold Stone Creamery, Pfizer, and Benjamin Moore all give away free samples of their product for promotional purposes. Each offers consumers a trial of its brand experience, confident that once a consumer tries its product the consumer will be back for more. Cold Stone Creamery offers free tastes of ice cream to ensure that you'll be happy with the flavor that you pick. Pfizer gives free drug samples, as well as clinical data and other marketing boons, to your doctor in hopes that that information (and your doctor's influence) will be passed on to you. You can take home as many paint chips as you can carry from Benjamin Moore, but you can also buy a small pot of paint for a nominal fee; the sample encourages decorators to paint a small patch of wall before they waste a day making a garish mistake. It is easy to see how samples may be advantageous to companies that sell a product, but how might this apply to libraries that already give their product away for free? How do you bottle the library experience?

Although there is no monetary cost associated with most library services, our users' time is just as valuable. The ability to try something makes doing easier. Patrons can try without fear. It is human nature to be a little afraid of new things. People often prefer to do what they know, thinking that it is easier, even if they get poor or inconsistent results and even if it takes longer. Think Google. There is an ancient Chinese proverb that states, "I hear, and I forget. I see, and I remember. I do, and I understand." When practice is added, learning is reinforced. Active learning is an instructional approach that encourages learner interaction and involvement. John Dewey was among the first to propose that experience plays an essential role in learning, ensuring that learners understand and retain knowledge.[2]

In the children's classic book *Caps for Sale*, Esphyr Slobodkina writes about a sleeping peddler whose caps are stolen by monkeys in a tree.[3] When the peddler wakes and discovers his hats are missing, he asks, yells at, and shakes his first at the monkeys, but they do not return the hats. The caps are returned only when the peddler throws the only cap he has left to the ground in frustration. When he throws his cap down, the monkeys do too. By extension, we are much more likely to try something when we have witnessed positive results from the action. We learn by example and from doing. In the development of sociocultural theory, Vygotsky establishes the significance of "conscious understanding" in a learning environment and describes the value of conscious imitation, where a learner's understanding is influenced by his or her perception of different elements and their relationship to one another.[4] Both of these learning theories are at work when libraries present advertising and learning activities and processes in a relevant, social context. This strategy has worked for us in the past with our Meebo IM service.

Meebo is a free, web-based IM program that supports multiple IM services, including AIM, Facebook Chat, Google Talk, NET Messenger Service, Yahoo!, and more. Meebo also features an anonymous widget that can be added to any web page. The Bryant University Library web site includes a Meebo widget in several places, including the library home page, the "Ask a Librarian" page, and subject guide pages. We also include a Meebo widget on external web sites that relate to library content, such as Facebook and Blackboard. The Meebo widget allows students to ask a reference question anonymously, but most importantly they can ask us a question without logging into their own IM. That's how we sell it to them. When our students have a question for a librarian, they are usually studying and may not want to be bothered by their friends. Meebo allows our users to IM a librarian without letting their friends know that they are online. It also sells itself by its convenient location. It is already on and it lives where they are. Users don't have to open another program or click on a pop up window.

When we began introducing and showing students how to use the Meebo widget in class, our statistics began to increase and they keep increasing. We don't just point to the widget; we type in a question or a greeting to the librarian on duty and wait for a response while we continue to describe the service. When students see the librarian respond, there is a collective, audible acknowledgement that indicates both understanding and excitement that it works. The popularity of Meebo is huge—the number of questions has more than doubled in one year. We do not keep detailed user statistics, but librarians who field Meebo questions believe that anonymous users outnumber those asking questions from their own IM accounts by approximately two to one.

It is easy to translate this same strategy for text messaging. In instruction classes, students should be urged to enter the text reference number in class. It can also become an assessment strategy—students can text a question that they still have after the end of an instruction session. After the session, it would be important for the library to answer every question seriously. At the reference desk, librarians can respond to students and follow-up with research requests by sending students text messages. Poll Everywhere (www.polleverywhere.com) is an easy-to-use text message voting application that is free for up to 32 users. It can be used with any live audience—in a classroom, discussion group, or presentations. People vote by sending text messages or using Twitter to options displayed on-screen. The poll updates in real time as voting results appear and the poll can be embedded within a presentation or a web page. Poll Everywhere is a great excuse for people to take their cell phones out and a way to reinforce the cell phone/library connection. At Bryant, students enjoy it, raving "It is like a game show" and "It is like American idol." It makes instruction sessions dynamic and encourages increased participation.

Henry Ford, the founder of the Ford Motor Company, is reported to have said, "If I had asked my customers what they wanted, they would have said a faster horse." Customers are not right if they do not know that what they want exists or is even possible. In a blog post entitled, "Apple's Secret? It Tells Us What We Should Love," Roberto Verganti writes about the iPad and Apple's approach to innovation. Led by Steve Jobs, Apple does not innovate based on what consumers want; they envision the ideal and then wait to see if consumers are ready.[5] At our university, students want Google. Do we give them what they want or do we teach them how to use something better? We can not wait for our users to demand services, we have to be one step ahead of them and be ready to fill the gap.

Bryant University officially launched the "Text a Librarian" service at the Douglas and Judith Krupp Library in October 2007. Since that time, the numbers have been increasing steadily. Text messaging enhances the quality of our outreach to our users. The number of total reference inquiries continues to rise at Bryant University. We believe that advertising is a way to get and keep our customers. When people like something, they recommend it to their friends. By winning one customer, you win his or her friends and your brand spreads. In essence, advertising is like a game of "Go Fish" where you collect as many ranks (customers) as you can. You win the game by collecting them all.

NOTES

1. *Field of Dreams*, DVD, directed by Phil Alden Robinson (1989; Los Angele, CA: Universal Studios, 2004).

2. John Dewey, *Experience and Education* (New York: Macmillan, 1938).

3. L. S. Vygotsky, *Thought and Language*, trans. Alex Kozulin (Cambridge: MIT Press, 1986).

4. Roberto Verganti, January 28, 2010, "Apple's secret? It tells us what we should love," *The Conversation,* accessed May 30, 2010, http://blogs.hbr.org/cs/2010/01/how_apple_innovates_by_telling. html.

5. Esphyr Slobodkina, *Caps for Sale—A Tale of a Peddler, a Monkey and Their Monkey Business* (New York: Scholastic Books, 1973).

Mobilizing the Library's Web Presence and Services: A Student-Library Collaboration to Create the Library's Mobile Site and iPhone Application

MATTHEW CONNOLLY
Olin Library, Cornell University, Ithaca, NY

TONY COSGRAVE
Uris Library, Cornell University, Ithaca, NY

BASEEMA B. KRKOSKA
Albert R. Mann Library, Cornell University, Ithaca, NY

The Library Outside the Library group collaborated with the Cornell University Library web site team and student programmers to mobilize the library, creating a mobile version of the library website and an iPhone/iPod touch application that bring library resources to handheld devices. A mobile version of the web site was developed using an open-source tool. Requests from mobile devices are translated according to custom rules and page filters. The iPhone application takes advantage of the iPhone's interface to present catalog searches, patron accounts, library hours, and other information in an intuitive way. Early responses to the mobile initiatives have been positive.

TAKING THE LIBRARY OUTSIDE THE LIBRARY

Cornell University Library's (CUL) Library Outside the Library (LOL) team works to make the library visible and usable outside of standard library places, tools, and services. To do this, it finds, configures, distributes, and assesses electronic tools and services that take the library to its users, wherever they may be. LOL has developed a lightweight approach to innovation: we leverage existing tools, providing local customizations when necessary; we foster a culture of experimentation and a willingness to discontinue unsuccessful projects; and we are not afraid to embrace what may be short-lived trends. After all, this is where many of our patrons are at the moment.

Our projects include a CUL iPhone/iPod Touch application and companion mobile version of our web site, reference services via Short Messaging Service (SMS), and several significant collections on Flickr. Some initiatives have proved so successful that they have been incorporated into core library functions and services.

WHY WE MOBILIZED

The LOL group is constantly looking for new ways to bring the library to our users. Public services staff regularly sees students using their handheld devices in the library. Students come up to the reference desks with call numbers on their screens and send questions to us using text messages. At the same time, many library staff members had handheld devices and were actively exploring mobile interfaces to information sources. It became clear that mobile access to the library was a topic worth investigating.

We talked with student representatives on the Student Library Advisory Council. This is a group of approximately 20 students, both graduates and undergraduates, who meet once a month to provide input on library issues. We showed them examples of mobile library projects from other libraries, including the New York Public Library and North Carolina State University Library, and they encouraged us to develop a mobile site for CUL. We also did some data mining on our web server logs and saw a 75% increase in the number of mobile devices accessing library servers during one semester (September 1–21, 2008: 138 views from iPod/iPhone, 3 views from other mobile devices; February 1–21, 2009: 5,844 views from iPod/iPhone, 4,676 views from other mobile devices). We were also monitoring listserves, blogs, and the various literature regarding mobile developments in libraries.

As a result of this data, we decided to develop two mobile versions of our content: a mobile-friendly interface to our standard web site and an iPhone/iPod touch application that accesses a subset of library services.

CUL MOBILE WEB SITE

Although we knew we wanted to develop an iPhone application for the library, we did not want to disenfranchise any of our users. Our student advisory council also recommended a device-neutral approach. Thus, we first began work on a version of our main web site (http://www.library.cornell.edu) that would be accessible to any mobile device.

There are multiple approaches to "mobilizing" a web site, and the number of tools for doing so has increased rapidly during the few months since we began this project. One technique would be to direct mobile users to a different set of content pages that provide different or simplified features. However, this forces the site owner to maintain two sets of distinct but overlapping content.

A second approach is to serve a single set of content to all patrons while using different style sheets or templates to reformat it for desktop or mobile browsers as appropriate. In our case, since we were running a Drupal-based site, there were several third-party modules available to help do just that. However, we felt that creating mobile-friendly templates for the many different content types and sections of our site would be too time-consuming (particularly because that variety and extent of that content might expand in the future).

A third alternative is to use a site transcoder: a rule-based interpreter that sits between a web site and a client, intercepting content as it is sent from the site to the client and reformatting it as needed for a mobile device. The promised advantage of this method is that it requires no changes to a site's content or styles/templates. Instead, a site owner creates a set of filters and rules that explicitly state how content is to be modified for mobile clients. This is the approach that we used to mobilize the CUL web site. After considering the available tools, we chose to go with Siruna (http://www.siruna.com). Although Siruna offers a "fully managed" option for creating mobile sites, it also provides an open-source, Java-based transcoder that can be installed and used on your own server (http://open.siruna.org).

To mobilize a site using Siruna, an administrator creates a new project and begins adding filters for that site. Each filter matches a particular URL or a subset of URLs. Each filter is assigned a number of rules that affect the formatting of content. Most rules make use of Siruna "transformers" that can optimize images, remove Javascript and CSS styles, rewrite links, reformat tables, or replace sections of HTML outright. Figure 1 shows a typical snippet of the rules code. The first line calls "CULTemplateCleaner," a common set of rules that strip out the header, footer, and other elements of the standard CUL template found on all site pages. The remaining lines remove specific elements of the content for the pages identified by that particular filter.

For the CUL web site, we chose to completely replace the home page content with a list of selected links to services (catalog search, Ask a Librarian, hours, events, staff directory, citation management, and a hand-picked list of mobile-friendly web sites) (http://www.library.cornell.edu/m) (Figure 2). Several other important content pages were given their own filters and rule sets to ensure that they would be usable on a mobile device. For

```
<map:call resource="CULTemplateCleaner" />
    <map:transform type="sirunaElementTransformer">
        <map:parameter name="task0" value="remove(//p:div[@id='gmap-auto2map-gmap0'])" />
        <map:parameter name="task1" value="remove(//p:div[@id='main']/p:div[6])" />
        <map:parameter name="task2" value="remove(//p:div[@id='main']/p:div[6]/p:div[6])" />
        <map:parameter name="task3"
value="remove(//p:div[@id='main']/p:div[6]/p:div[1]/p:div[1]/p:div[2]/p:div[1]/p:div[1])" />
        <map:parameter name="task4" value="remove(//p:div[@id='main']/p:div[5])" />
    </map:transform>
```

FIGURE 1 Sample filter rules code used by Siruna.

the rest of the site content, we configured a default set of rules that would at least provide a basic level of mobile compatibility. Siruna also runs all page content through a basic set of cleanup filters by default. Finally, to search CUL's Voyager OPAC, we adopted a mobile Voyager theme developed at the University of Rochester that runs separately from the Siruna service and is accessed via one of the home page links.

Even though the mobile version of the CUL site is relatively simple and plain, it has received only positive feedback from library staff and patrons. We are currently working to analyze and evaluate use of the mobile site.

CUL IPHONE APP

Each fall semester, students from a computer science class (CS 5150: Software Engineering) put out a call for project proposals. Over the course of the semester, the CS 5150 students design and implement real-world projects for real-world clients at Cornell University. The library has worked with students from this class before and has been quite satisfied with the projects. The library was concerned about spending its staff time on an iPhone app knowing that it would privilege one category of users. However, at the same time, we were aware that other parts of the University were creating iPhone apps and that these devices are very popular with students, faculty, and staff on campus. We decided to submit a proposal to the students in CS 5150. Our proposal included a description of some desired features for a library iPhone app, but we purposely left room for the students to make suggestions of their own.

The whole process was handled in a very professional manner. The students were to treat us as real-world clients. They wrote a formal prospectus. They met every week with library staff to report their progress and listen to feedback. The students, their professor, and the library team met several times throughout the semester for the students to give formal presentations detailing their progress. Along the way, the library's usability group conducted formal usability studies with a prototype version of the app. This gave the students and library staff valuable feedback that was used to improve

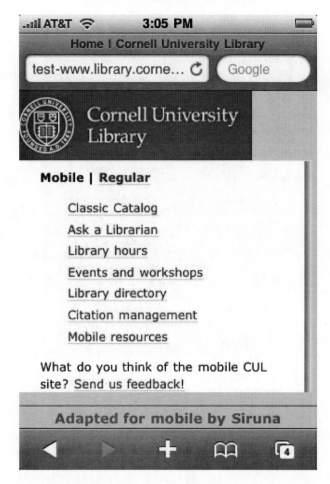

FIGURE 2 Mobile version of the CUL home page.

the app. In the end, the students gave us a working iPhone/iPod Touch application that includes the following features:

- Search access to the library catalog.
- Access to patron accounts.
- Listing of library hours and current status.
- Contact information for CUL unit libraries.
- Interactive campus/library map.
- Ask a Librarian.
- Links to mobile-friendly websites and resources.

The home screen of the app is shown in Figure 3.

The library catalog and patron account functions connect to CUL's Voyager OPAC to perform searches and retrieve information about the

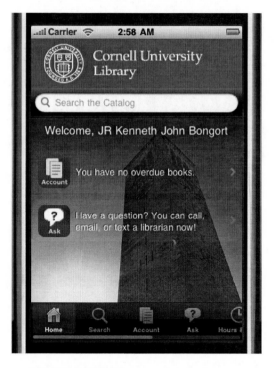

FIGURE 3 CUL iPhone app, home screen.

user's charged items, item requests, and any incurred fines or fees. From the account feature, a user may also renew a book or cancel a pending item request. The search feature allows catalog searches by title, author, or keyword. Search results include item availability and basic bibliographic information (Figure 4). Users can also recall an item.

We were fortunate in that the beginning of the iPhone development project coincided with CUL's transition to Voyager 7, which for the first time provided APIs for accessing the search functionality and patron records that we needed for this project. These come in the form of XML web services, designed to enable the creation of an alternate OPAC.

The Ask a Librarian option provides contact information for each of CUL's libraries when the app is used on an iPod touch. If the user has an iPhone, the phone, e-mail, and SMS links will activate the appropriate iPhone applications to actually perform those functions.

The library hours and map features integrate information about current library hours with a Google map, indicating which libraries are open and closed in real time (Figure 5). Using the map, users may find the nearest library open at a given time and contact the circulation or reference desks there.

Finally, the mobile links mirror the list of links provided for the mobile CUL site. It includes links to mobile-friendly databases and reference works,

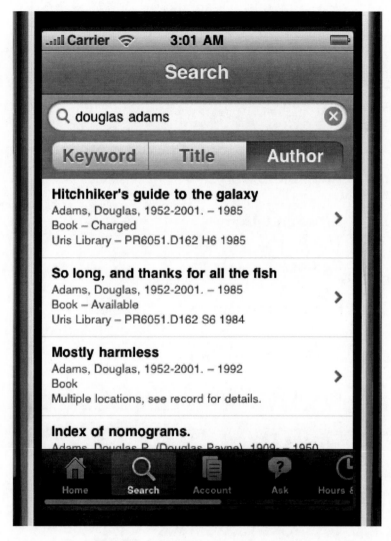

FIGURE 4 CUL iPhone app, search results.

free mobile web sites, and CUL's presence on such as like Flickr and Facebook.

One issue that we struggled with during the development of the app, and one that we still have not resolved to our satisfaction, is the problem of authentication for patron account data and connecting to licensed databases. Cornell's main site authentication system, CUWebAuth, is the method of choice by default, being used throughout the university and the library. However, during our development, it was not available in mobile form, nor was it permissible to store a user's CUWebAuth credentials in the app's settings. The current app uses a library-specific patron identifier that can be

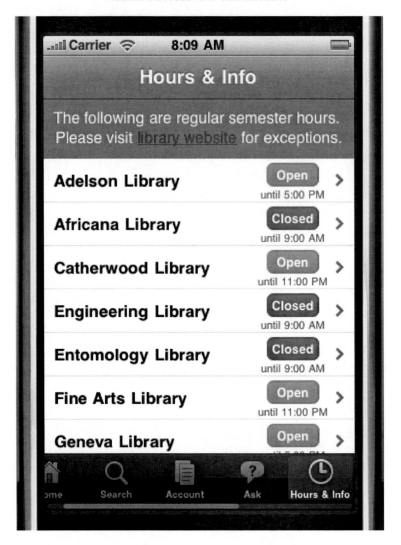

FIGURE 5 CUL iPhone app, hours.

set once by the user and ignored thereafter. However, this will have to be revisited in the near future as CUL moves away from this approach out of privacy concerns.

When the app was complete, the library undertook an aggressive advertising campaign. We designed posters and table tents. We ran news stories in two campus publications. We advertised on the Library and Cornell Information Technologies websites and created a YouTube video (http://www.youtube.com/watch?v=-ygOBpAY7WA).

The CUL iPhone app was submitted to Apple's iTunes store. Since being accepted and listed there, it has been downloaded more than 800 times and has an average rating of four of five stars. Customer feedback has been very positive, including comments such as "beautiful. period." and "a truly beautiful app . . . . Actually amazing!!"

The app can be downloaded for free at the iTunes store (http://itunes. apple.com/us/app/cu-library/id354721654?mt=8).

FUTURE PLANS

Even though we are happy with the success of our new mobile services, we do have a wish list of future enhancements, some of which came from the Student Library Advisory Council when the new app was presented to them. We are interested in adding the Qwidget that we use for our chat reference services. We would also like to incorporate our LibGuides, course reserves, and library events into the iPhone app.

We are currently in the process of hiring the student who served as the team leader for the CS 5150 team to maintain the iPhone app and expand its features. We are also considering submitting another proposal to the CS 5150 class to see if we can interest another team in working for the library. This could potentially lead to a new app, enhancements to our current app, or perhaps even an iPad version.

But as we look to the future of our Library's mobile presence, we are also considering a more device-independent approach. This seems like a potentially more efficient way to meet the current and future needs of our mobile library users as the variety and use of advanced mobile devices grows.

Collaborative Marketing for Virtual Reference: The My Info Quest Experience

BETH FUSELER AVERY
University of North Texas Libraries, Denton, TX

KAREN J. DOCHERTY
Maricopa Community Colleges/Rio Salado College, Tempe, AZ

MARY-CAROL LINDBLOOM
South Central Regional Library Council, Ithaca, NY

This article shares general information about the My Info Quest collaborative, explores publicity for the cooperative and how the public relations committee developed materials for participating libraries and the public, and details how marketing has occurred at the local level.

INTRODUCTION

Librarians have a long history of cooperation, including the sharing of physical library materials and calling on one another for ideas and advice. Opportunities to collaborate increased as consortia developed and expanded. Although reference expertise was shared long before the first collaborative virtual reference service emerged, this type of service took cooperation to a new level as librarians began to provide information directly to each others' users on an hourly basis.

The Alliance Library System of East Peoria, Illinois, was one of the first library consortia to explore virtual reference service. Its Library Services and

Technology Act-funded virtual reference pilot project, *Ready for Reference*, brought together eight academic library members. After a year, *Ready for Reference* merged with North Suburban Library System's public library virtual reference initiative, *Answers Unlimited*, to form MyWebLibrarian, forming a multitype service. MyWebLibrarian in turn expanded and merged with Illinois' statewide AskAwayIllinois virtual reference service. Members of MyWebLibrarian's advisory committee participated in the planning, development, and implementation of AskAwayIllinois.

With their experience in virtual reference service implementation in an environment of increasing use of mobile devices and SMS texting, it was a natural undertaking for Alliance Library System to explore point-of-need collaborative information assistance for the growing number of text messagers. The numbers are increasing dramatically. A Pew Internet and American Life study published in April 2010 (Lenhart et al. 2010) indicated that 72% of teens (of 88% of teens using cell phones) use text, which is up from 51% in 2006. Jenna Wortham (2010) reported in *The New York Times* that households are increasingly severing their landline connections and going mobile. Furthermore, data transmission now exceeds the amount of voice data.

Key reasons to collaborate in virtual reference provision have been to share expertise, ideas, experiences, and strategies; to develop best practices, standards, and guidelines; to share desk rotations; to offer more hours of desk service than any one library could staff; to share and leverage costs; to share a web site and marketing; and, above all else, to provide point-of-need help to library users and would-be library users. All of the benefits of virtual reference collaboration carry over to text reference.

The resulting service, My Info Quest: Txt 4 Answers, had several charter partners, including Altarama (which has provided the software to channel incoming text messages to a shared email account), Web Clarity Software Inc. (which initially provided Peoplewhere for scheduling), San Jose State University Graduate School of Library and Information Science, South Central Regional Library Council in New York, and TAP Information Services. The first organizational meeting was held early in 2009; the service went "live" in July 2009, with a few dozen libraries/systems participating. Nearly a year later, approximately 70 libraries/systems from all over the United States participate; My Info Quest recently welcomed its first Canadian partner. The pilot project phase is financially supported through December 2010 and will shift to participant-sustained funding in 2011.

An advisory group comprised of participating libraries meets monthly to review and evaluate progress, as well as to address issues. In addition, there are several working groups, including standards and guidelines, training, and marketing/public relations.

Requirements of participation are minimal. Participating libraries are asked to place a link on their web site and publicize the service to their communities, have a representative on the advisory group, initially attend training sessions and practice sessions, contribute to the evaluation of the service, staff the desk two hours per week, and communicate via the project's Google Group.

My Info Quest is available to all users of the participating libraries by texting to the service's telephone number or pointing their mobile device's camera to the Quick Response (QR) code. The service answers most of the questions received and has a disclaimer about not providing medical, tax, or legal advice. Librarians do not need to know how to text to participate; in fact, responding to questions has the "feel" of e-mail with two caveats: (1) answers are limited to 320 characters and (2) librarians strive to answer questions within ten minutes. From July 2009 through April 2010, My Info Quest librarians have answered 6,694 questions. The service is open 83 hours per week, with the goal of 24/7/365 availability.

As with virtual reference, text reference enhances traditional references services—it is one additional way to connect with library users and other members of our communities to offer them assistance at their point-of-need. Anne Grodzins Lipow's (1999) quote, "rather than thinking of our users as remote, we should instead recognize that we are remote from our users" (51), uttered in the context of structuring our services to connect with them in their environment, applies to the world of mobile devices. Cooperating to achieve this is a cost-effective and realistic way to accomplish this and expand our reach.

PUBLICITY FOR THE COOPERATIVE

Because My Info Quest is a cooperative reference service project, we realized early on that we needed a consistent message both for libraries and the public. Many of the libraries who joined the original group were small and had limited resources for developing publicity items. A public relations committee was formed to develop these marketing messages and items that libraries could use in their publicity efforts.

Talking Points

Although text reference service was not brand new, it was still new enough that many libraries had not considered it as a way to provide reference even though many of our patrons were devoted cell phone texters. Therefore, among the early items developed were two talking points documents: one for recruiting libraries into the consortium and one for the public to know what the service was all about.

The Talking Points for Libraries document was designed to be an easy place to get answers to the questions we knew potential member libraries would ask. It also served as a quick reference document that those of us who were recruiting could access to build a case for joining. It answered the following basic questions:

- What is My Info Quest? This was important because we were recruiting all types and sizes of libraries. Many of the libraries were not familiar with this service and we wanted a brief way to describe it.
- How much does it cost? In today's economy, this is of primary importance to most libraries. We wanted to reassure potential members right away that it was not expensive.
- Do we need a cell phone to participate? This it turns out was a critical question for many libraries. Although most of the patrons had cell phones, many libraries did not. Librarians did not want to have to use their own cell phones, especially if they paid for each text message. In addition, many libraries weren't ready to buy cell phones for reference use.
- How many hours does my library have to staff it? Another important question as library staffs are being cut. We needed people to know that this would not become an onerous project.
- What else does my library have to do? This question covered all the other time, technology, and money issues. It included links on the library's web site, publicizing to their patrons, training time needed, and communication issues.
- What are the hours of service? Our ultimate goal was 24/7 service, but with a limited number of libraries participating we could not staff that much at first. So, we were upfront about the hours being modest to start and hoping that they would expand quickly.
- Who is the audience? As the committee discussed this, we realized that it was not just the younger population that was texting, it was everyone from young to old. It just depended on the penetration of texting in the library's service population.
- How are decisions made about the service? Governance of all cooperative projects is always a concern. We wanted to reassure each library that it could have a voice in the running and continuance of the service.

The Talking Points for Patrons document was designed to give librarians a starting point to talk to their users about this new service. We wanted to provide an idea of what they could expect because they would be talking to librarians who were not in "their" library, so setting appropriate expectations would be important to getting user buy-in.

- What is My Info Quest? At the point we started in July 2009, there weren't many text-for-answer type services. We wanted a basic description of the service.

- Who can use the service? We wanted to emphasize that they could use the service because their home library was participating in the project.
- How do I contact My Info Quest? Because we were going to track usage by using a library code for the patron's home library, it was important that they knew to include that three-letter code at the start of their message and, of course, that they had the telephone number in their cell phone.
- What kind of questions can I ask? Because people might see this as different than the types of questions they would ask at their home library, we wanted them to know that any questions were accepted, but that they had to ask in 160 characters or less.
- We cannot answer questions about your library account or renew books. Patrons needed to know up front that we did not have access to their library records, and therefore we would not be able to help them with renewing books.
- What does it cost? Although the answers were free, many people at that time did not have unlimited texting on their telephones. Therefore, people needed to know that, if they were charged per message, their cell phone provider might charge for each message.
- How soon will I get an answer? Because we were not answering questions 24/7, people needed to know both how soon they would get an answer when we were staffed and what would happen when we were not staffed.
- Will my messages be private? Since privacy is of primary importance to libraries and their people, we wanted the patrons to know that text messaging is not entirely secure and that we would save the questions for a short period of time for quality control.
- Who is answering my questions? Again, we emphasized that this was a cooperative of over 60 libraries.

Creating a Tagline

The committee realized that the name My Info Quest might not totally convey the way this reference service operated. Therefore, we thought we would try to develop a tagline that would enhance the service name by inviting ideas from patrons.

First, we had a call for possible taglines and asked libraries to engage their users in this process. Libraries solicited input from student workers, book clubs, library groupies, other groups (student or otherwise), and individuals who might have fun with this. We received 18 possible taglines, from short ("txt lib") to long ("Need Info? Answers just a txt away!").

Next, we sent out a survey to the My Info Quest participants, asking for the top three choices for a tagline. To get an idea of what would appeal to a wide range of groups, we loosely used the age breakdown from the Pew Internet & American Life generational studies. We placed the Leading and

Trailing Boomers age categories together, combined the Silent and GI, and expanded the under 17 group to include children as young as 10.

We also asked the status of the responder: Librarian/Library Director/ Library Worker (90.0%, 81 responses), Student Worker (3.3%, 3 responses), Library Volunteer (1.1%, 1 response), Library User (4.4%, 4 responses), and Other (1.1%, 1 response)

We quickly realized a long tagline for a quick short question did not make sense and the survey confirmed this. From the four top taglines, the committee selected "txt 4 answers."

Traditional Marketing Methods

Traditional methods often work the best. Several possible publicity pieces were discussed, including bookmarks and postcards. We also discussed the necessity in a cooperative setting for each library to be able to customize materials for its own environment.

Book marks were created in MS Word so that libraries that do not have access to or expertise with using many tools could usually easily modify the document. The front of the bookmark has the My Info Quest logo, the tagline, the web site URL, and the telephone number in the largest letters. The back of the book mark was designed to be easily customized. It had three lines of text: "You can text your questions anytime. Messages will be answered {INSERT CURRENT DAY AND HOUR INFORMATION HERE} Central time. A service brought to you by: {INSERT YOUR LIBRARY INFORMATION HERE}." There is also enough white space for the library to include its logo.

The committee realized that most libraries do not have public relations staff and that they would want to have something to send to local papers, use as a radio public service announcement, or include in a library newsletter. We developed a short news blurb:

> On the go and need an answer? Text your question to our library and have the answer delivered to your phone in any zone with **My Info Quest: txt 4 answers**! Here's how:
>
> Call 309-222-7740 and enter your library's code
>
> Txt your question
>
> A librarian will text an expert answer within minutes during the hours of service, XXXX.
>
> It's easy and accurate! For more information, visit www.myinfoquest.info. My Info Quest is brought to you by the XXX Library.

TABLE 1 Checklist for Semester Start-up Marketing Ideas

Links to service: Placement is critical to success of service
Library and school web pages
  ✓ consistent spot
  ✓ consistent logo/message
  ✓ multiple access points
Courseware pages, such as WebCT, Angel, Blackboard
Instructor class web pages
Can online databases can be customized to include a link to your VR Service?
Create a tag line for your email signature
Inserts for bookstore
Flyer for bathroom stalls, stairwells, building entry doors, residence halls
Message magnets for bathroom stalls
Table tents for cafeteria and library tables
Inserts for freshman orientation packets
bookmarks for freshmen
Inserts for bookstore
After hours message for phone
Cafeteria take-out inserts or napkins
Information for college vans and buses
Library newsletter, newspapers, TV shows, radio
Message magnets for bathroom stalls
Message for electronic announcement boards, kiosks, sporting events boards
Scrolling monitor messages in computer labs, screensavers
Signs in carrels, on end caps, book drops
Faculty back-to-school meeting packets
Registration desks

As more academic libraries came into the project, the committee members realized that they would have to publicize the service every semester and that a checklist would be handy to help them remember what to do. After it was developed, we realized that many of the items on the list would be useful for any library beginning to publicize the service, and so we created the checklist (Table 1).

The checklist included the ideas the committee developed during a brainstorming session and is intended to be a starting point for institutions to begin thinking about how they will market the service in their particular setting.

As the project continues, the committee has been compiling the best of the publicity being done by member libraries and continues to develop additional publicity pieces for all member libraries to use.

MARKETING MY INFO QUEST AT THE LOCAL LEVEL

Rio Salado College, one of the ten Maricopa Community Colleges based in the Phoenix metropolitan area, began offering and promoting My Info Quest in early fall of 2009. One of the Maricopa sister colleges, Paradise

Valley Community College, is also a pilot participant, but the focus of this article will be on the marketing experiences of Rio Salado College because of this author's first-hand involvement in the following efforts.

There are several demographics that make a text messaging service a viable service delivery option for Rio Salado College. We have a large population of approximately 13,000 FTSE (full-time student equivalent), with a total headcount of 61,340 students based on 2008–2009 data, of which a substantial segment is made up of online students. Rio Salado College also has many dual enrollment (high school) students, a user group that is likely to be heavy text messagers based on the results from the Pew Internet & American Life study, "Teens and Mobile Phones," in which the authors state, "text messaging has become the primary way that teens reach their friends, surpassing face-to-face contact, email, instant messaging and voice calling as the go-to daily communication tool for this age group" (Lenhart et al. 2010). Because we currently serve this teen segment and anticipate serving many more in this demographic in the years ahead, we were motivated to investigate texting as a service option.

The Marketing Roll Out

Rio Salado College decided to start with a soft roll out of the My Info Quest service, which we locally named "Ask! Txt 4 Answers" to better parallel our existing chat service named Ask a Librarian. We did not want a giant marketing push since it was an unproven service. We really were not sure how reliable it would be and the level of quality that students could expect. Although we were interested in exploring texting as way to provide reference, we were not convinced that it would be the right delivery mode for our academic environment given texting's inherent character limitations. Plus, we were not sure how long we were going to participate in the pilot. Therefore, we started small by adding an icon to our web site that linked to a secondary page that provided more information about the service, including the telephone number, library code, hours of service, and a blurb about the types of questions that are best suited for the service.

Marketing Approaches

Rio Salado's former college president loved innovative ideas and was pleased to highlight the collaborative text messaging pilot during her State of the College address to all faculty and staff during fall semester 2009. Her mention of the service led to interest in the service from our Institutional Advancement (IA) office, a proactive group of staff members who employ creative approaches to promoting the college. An IA staff member wrote an article highlighting Ask! Txt 4 Answers that appeared in various local city editions of our newspaper, *The Arizona Republic* (Staudacher 2009). The same article also appeared on the AZFamily.com web site, the companion web site of local channel 3TV. Although I might not have felt ready to spread the word about the service, the IA group was so we went with it.

To promote the service internally, the IA staff also posted the same article on our college-wide staff portal as a news item. It is always important to make sure your colleagues are aware of the services you provide, so they can help to promote it to the students they encounter.

The IA staff also included Ask! Txt 4 Answers on one of the most heavily visited student pages on the Rio Salado web site—our Current Students' page. They highlighted the service as one of the student-focused enhancements for the 2008–2009 academic year and included a link to the library site. Brief information about the service also appeared in RioLounge, Rio Salado's own social networking site.

In addition to newspaper and web site articles and links for both internal and external promotion, the Rio Salado instruction librarian began mentioning the service to the multitude of dual enrollment high school classes she visits in person. She has reported that some students have noticed the service on their own and have asked about it, and that their responses have elicited exclamations of "cool." We know from our ongoing and extensive experience tracking patron exit surveys with our 24/7 chat service, Ask a Librarian, that promotion by a trusted librarian or instructor is second in effectiveness only to finding a service through links on a web site.

Continuing on the theme of word of mouth promotion by a trusted source, one important key to the success of our chat service has been making faculty aware of it and encouraging them to tell their students about it. For chat we have created special marketing messages and giveaways just for faculty, visited department meetings, and included information and items in adjunct faculty packets. The same needs to happen for promoting the texting service. If students know that their instructors endorse the service, they will use it. If students know they should use the library and are encouraged to ask questions, they will.

Other ideas for promoting the service include mentioning the service and telephone number on circulation slips and other take away items—the types of things someone might put in a wallet or a backpack and have handy when they want to send a text message, such as a business card. Posters or table tents for those spaces where computers may not be available are also a good idea: group study rooms, study carrels, the cafeteria, classrooms, hallways, and tutoring centers.

Most importantly, any signage or promotional items must include a message to add the service number to one's mobile device contacts list. Because the need for service may not arise when the patron is at a computer and able to have ready access to a web site with information about the service, it would be most helpful to already have the number handy. Besides, if a student is at a computer, he or she may likely use other service options, such as chat or instant messaging.

Future Considerations

Having already implemented a few promotional strategies, we still have very low usage, especially compared to the success of our live chat service. From the months of September 2009 through April 2010, Rio Salado College and Paradise Valley Community College patrons' usage accounted for only 49 text transactions. This is low when compared to the 1,554 chat transactions from these two colleges for the same time frame. The overall My Info Quest service itself continues to enjoy growth with an average range of 800 to 1,000 questions per month from all participating libraries.

So what accounts for the low usage and is it worth it to continue with the service? We have several ideas for why the statistics are so low. (1) With chat, students are likely online using the library web site, so if they have a question, the natural flow is to click on a chat button or to start chatting in a widget and it is less likely for the student to pick up a separate device and text a question. (2) At the moment when texting would be most beneficial, the telephone number and library code are not available. This is why it is so important that all promotional material contain these numbers along with a message about adding the number to one's contacts list. (3) Students see texting as social and do not wish to use it for course-related work. (4) Students know the character limitations of texting and recognize that a different access mode, such as in-person help, telephone, or chat, may be more appropriate for their information need. (5) More promotion is needed.

In the early days of our chat service, usage was also very low. It took deliberate effort over the course of time to get the word out to faculty and students that the service is available. With a continually changing student body, marketing efforts never cease. A commitment to provide the service must also entail a commitment to promote it. Many of the activities mentioned in Checklist for Semester Start-up Marketing Ideas are worth pursuing.

Despite our initial low usage and concerns about the lack of ability to provide instruction in a text environment, Rio Salado College is likely to continue to offer a texting service. The opportunity to reach out to a large group of students who are comfortable with this form of communication makes a compelling case for its ongoing viability. Not all questions will be answered with texting but some will be, and for the others, the chance to establish positive contact with students and help move them in the right direction is worth the effort.

REFERENCES

Lenhart, Amanda, Rich Ling, Scott Campbell, and Kirsten Purcell. 2010. "Teens and Mobile Phones." Pew Internet & American Life Project. Accessed August 16, 2010. http://www.pewinternet.org/Reports/2010/Teens-and-Mobile-Phones.aspx.

Lipow, Anne Grodzins. 1999. "'In Your Face' Reference Service." *Library Journal* 124: 51.

Staudacher, David. 2009. "Have a Question? Text a Librarian." *Arizona Republic*, November 14.

Wortham, Jenna. 2010. "Cellphones Now Used More for Data than for Calls." *The New York Times*, May 13. Accessed August 16, 2010. http://www.nytimes.com/2010/05/14/technology/personaltech/14talk.html.

From Internet to iPhone: Providing Mobile Geographic Access to Philadelphia's Historic Photographs and other Special Collections

DEBORAH BOYER

Azavea, Philadelphia, PA

PhillyHistory.org contains more than 95,000 map and photographic records from the City of Philadelphia Department of Records and other local institutions, searchable and viewable by geographic location and other criteria. The Department of Records further expanded public access capabilities through the release of PhillyHistory.org optimized for smartphones, enabling users to view historic photos of a location as they stroll the streets of Philadelphia. PhillyHistory.org serves as a case study for how libraries can use mobile technologies to increase access to their special collections and provide learning opportunities that transcend the traditional web site.

BACKGROUND

Since the late 1800s, the City of Philadelphia has used photography to record the growth and progress of the city. Photographers employed by various city departments traveled through dozens of neighborhoods to document everything from architecture and schools to local events and construction projects. Although these images were often captured before and after public works projects as a risk management tool, the unintended side effect was the creation of an incredibly rich 140-year visual history of Philadelphia's streets, industry, culture, and people. With images of everything from the Sesquicentennial Exposition of 1926 to the construction of City Hall to pretzel vendors outside a local high school, this collection of more than one million photographs is an amazing resource for scholars, students, Philadelphians, and anyone interested in history.

The majority of the images are held by the Philadelphia City Archives under the administration of the City of Philadelphia's Department of Records (DOR). Although these images were available to the public, the DOR wished to address the following problems:

1. Organization. Many of the negatives were not cataloged, and specific individual images were often difficult to locate.
2. Preservation. Although the negatives are housed in a climate-controlled secure space, many of the images were stored in their original acidic envelopes and faced chemical and physical degradation.
3. Access. Although the City Archives is open to the public, access to the photographic collection was limited; many of the images had not been seen since the negatives were developed.
4. Funding. Due to budget restrictions, any photo project needed to be both sustainable and a possible source of revenue.

The combination of all these factors meant that any proposed solution needed to develop a process for digitizing and organizing the collection, create a method for managing the metadata related to the images, and improve public access to the images—all while generating revenue.

To address these issues, the DOR created *Philly*History.org (www. phillyhistory.org), an online database that provides free public access to digitized images from the collection of the Philadelphia City Archives and other area institutions (see Figure 1). The web site provided the DOR with the means to increase accessibility to the images, organize and preserve the physical negatives, digitize the images as a preservation measure, and generate revenue via print sales. In the process, they sought public involvement and feedback and have gradually created a consortium of Philadelphia organizations seeking to make their collections more available with geographic search capabilities.

At the beginning of the project, the DOR realized that many of the images were associated with a location, such as an address or intersection. The DOR felt that this connection to place would resonate with potential users of the site. People connect strongly with the built environment, and historic places can trigger memories for many individuals.[1] Because Philadelphia has long been known as a city of neighborhoods, the DOR reasoned that people would want to locate images based on geographic criteria, such as address, intersection, or neighborhood. Enabling users to easily find and purchase a historic print of their neighborhood also tied into the necessity of having a revenue generating component to the site.

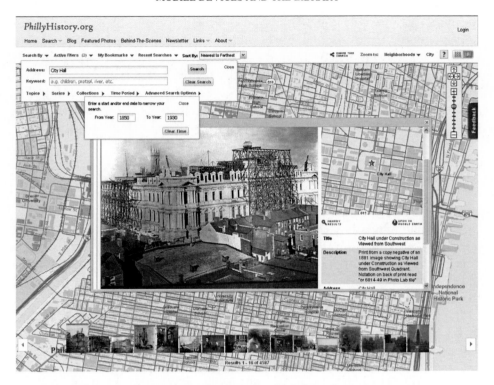

FIGURE 1 *Philly*History.org search page.

However, geographic search functions proved to be uncommon in database software. To develop a site that would feature such an option, the DOR partnered with Azavea, a Philadelphia-based software company specializing in Geographic Information Systems (GIS) technology. Azavea created Sajara, the web-based geographic digital asset management software that powers *Philly*History.org. Featuring both a public side and administrative side, *Philly*History.org helped the DOR make the images available to the public while also providing administrative management tools for Archives staff.

Over the next several years, the DOR and Azavea continued to add new features to *Philly*History.org. The public can now contribute error reports, request scans of missing photos, leave comments, tag their favorite photographs, be notified when new images are added (thanks to RSS feeds), and enjoy special features such as viewing the images in Google Earth and Google Street View. These tools furthered the goals of increasing public interaction with these historic photos and helping people connect with the City Archives collections, Philadelphia's history, and, for many, their families' histories.

Although the database began with only 90 images in 2005, it has grown to contain more than 95,000 records from five organizations—the Philadelphia Department of Records, the Philadelphia Water Department, the Free Library of Philadelphia, the Philadelphia Office of the City Representative, and the Library Company of Philadelphia. With many cultural institutions facing resource issues, *Philly*History.org provides an opportunity for organizations to share the burdens and benefits of providing digital access to their collections. A system of watermarks, customizable metadata fields, and varying levels of administrative access enable organizations to display and manage their own assets while a unified search page provides the public with access to images from every collection.

Since its creation, *Philly*History.org has received strong positive feedback from the public, both in Philadelphia and throughout the United States. As one user said, "You help me remember my past. I see parts of the city as I was growing up and think of how things have changed. Thank you." The web site regularly receives 10,000 to 15,000 unique visitors a month and generates monthly print sales and license requests. In 2007, *Philly*History.org was awarded a Best of Philly award, as well as the URISA Exemplary Systems in Government award; in 2008, the site received the Henry Magaziner award from the American Institute of Architects of Philadelphia for its contribution to the preservation of the built environment. Although *Philly*History.org has faced some obstacles, including an ever-tightening budget and the necessity of spending time developing collaboration efforts, providing increased access to thousands of historic images has proven to be an immense success and an excellent way to help the public learn more about the history of their city.

MOVING TO MOBILE TECHNOLOGY

After several years of providing access to *Philly*History.org via a web-based application, the DOR investigated the possibility of making the photos available using mobile phones. Providing the images via mobile technology seemed an obvious extension of the project's focus on increased public access, as well as an ideal method for further emphasizing the geographic component of the photographs.

In summer 2007, the Department of Records launched *Philly*History.org Mobile. Accessible via cell phone, handheld computers, and other Internet capable mobile devices, the mobile application provided *Philly*History.org users with the option for viewing the historic images while walking near the location where they originally were taken. People could truly connect the past to the present and relate to the images from the Philadelphia City Archives in an entirely new and exciting way.

After the advent of smartphones in 2008 and 2009, the DOR began investigating how *Philly*History.org Mobile could be updated for use on the new generation of cell phones that included cameras, GPS radios, accelerometers and electronic compasses, including Google Android and

FIGURE 2 A mobile-optimized web application enables users to visit *Philly*History.org on their smartphones.

Apple iPhone. In 2009, Azavea, the software company who built the *Philly*History.org web application, created a smartphone version of the web application that provided access to the site via Apple iPhone and Google Android devices (see Figure 2).

To do so, the project team investigated several methods for building the mobile app, including adjusting the existing site and creating a native iPhone application for publication through the Apple App Store. Although native applications have access to more of the smartphone's capabilities, the team avoided the native app route and decided to create a web application tailored visually and functionally to the iPhone and Android phones' layout and interface. Using this method enabled quicker development time and allowed the application to be available for multiple phone platforms without having to create and maintain multiple applications. Since then, proliferating mobile platform technologies have become an increasing concern. Today, smartphone use is split between the iPhone, Android, BlackBerry, and Windows Mobile platforms, each requiring its own specific software development technology. A few technologies have appeared that attempt to bridge the multiple platforms, including the open source PhoneGap project, Adobe Flash, and Rhodes but recent moves by Apple to block many such cross-platform development technologies have cast doubt on the ability to create apps (other than web apps) that will function on all of the major platforms. Although this uncertainty has vindicated the *Philly*History team's decision to develop a mobile-optimized web application, it is a substantial concern for future development of engaging and useful mobile applications that will be available to the largest possible audience.

Creating a smartphone application for *Philly*History.org (available at http://phillyhistory.org/i/) was not simply a matter of reconfiguring the existing site. The small screen size of the telephone inevitably mandates that the features of the application be stripped down to the most important ones. Although all of the images in the database are available via the mobile app, geographic search is the only search function. Because the application is meant to be used while travelling throughout Philadelphia, forgoing the other search features does not appear to be too inconvenient. The application follows the general one screen per function design guideline for apps, enabling users to have a full screen view of each image. The application also leverages the location sensors in contemporary smartphones. If a phone has an available internal GPS system, a user can simply go to the *Philly*History.org site and the app will automatically load photos of the current location.

THE BENEFITS OF MOBILE TECHNOLOGY FOR SPECIAL COLLECTIONS

Providing mobile access to *Philly*History.org has proven to be an extremely useful tool for connecting users to the history of the city in an innovative and very immediate way. Viewing historic images of a site may help a student learn about the history of their city or enable an architect to examine the details that once existed on a building, but viewing those images while standing in the location where they were taken 100 years previously provides a powerful visual context that reinforces the connections between the past and the present. Many images depict buildings that no longer exist, so viewing those images via a smartphone is a compelling method for demonstrating how a location has changed. For example, *Philly*History.org includes a collection of images from the Centennial Exhibition Collection of the Free Library of Philadelphia. Fairmount Park, the location of the Centennial, was a bustling area filled with people and huge buildings in 1876, but the same locale is now a green space with only a few structures remaining. Using the *Philly*History.org mobile app, an individual can stand in the middle of Fairmount Park and virtually time travel back to the Centennial to see the buildings as they were more than 125 years ago.

Mobile technologies also have many potential benefits for the special collections held by libraries and other cultural institutions. Mobile applications can help many of these collections, ranging from photographs to maps to local history items, to reach new audiences, create additional learning and access opportunities, and redraw the geographic boundaries of a library collection. Similar to *Philly*History.org, many of these digital collections focus on the geography of the images and use mobile technology to help individuals compare past and present views of a location. Paired with audio recordings associated with the assets, these mobile systems redefine museum and special library collections by literally bringing assets beyond the walls of the institutions and into the streets. North Carolina State University (NCSU) recently developed a mobile project called WolfWalk that provides users with access to historic images from the NCSU Libraries Special Collections Research Center. WolfWalk enables users to access information and photographs for over ninety sites on the NCSU campus via mobile technology.[2] The Duke University Libraries have also made 32,000 images from 20 collections available via the DukeMobile applications for iPhone.[3]

Such projects demonstrate how libraries can use mobile technology to introduce their users to previously underused resources. Mobile technology can help an organization reach out to visitors who may have never visited the library's physical location. It can also help reinforce the library as a source of information for the local community and the far-flung digital community.

The increasing prevalence of mobile smartphones, tablet computers, and other portable Internet accessible devices ensures that many of the visitors to cultural institutions increasingly will come to expect immediate access to collections and information. *InformationWeek* estimated that, as of February 2010, there were approximately 45.4 million people in the United States who owned smartphones.[4] Teenagers in particular are embracing the use of cell phones for activities other than making phone calls. According to the Pew Internet & American Life Project, in April 2010 approximately 75% of those 12 to 17 years old owned cell phones. Among teenagers who own cell phones, 88% use the cell phones to send text messages and 27% to go online for a variety of purposes.[5]

Libraries and other cultural organizations are addressing this shift to mobile technology through a variety of projects and initiatives. David Ferriero, the Archivist of the United States, recently challenged the staff at the National Archives to consider how they can utilize mobile technology, such as mobile apps, applications specifically for archives datasets, and a staff networking application.[6] Other organizations have already developed mobile apps that focus on providing access to their catalogues or reference desks.

Although these catalog-based applications are vitally important for connecting libraries and other institutions to the needs of their patrons, providing mobile access to special collections can introduce entirely new audiences to previously unknown materials and reinforce the library as an educational and informational resource. By introducing a geographic component, these institutions can literally bring to life the physical environment of the cities and towns they service. However, before engaging in a mobile technology initiative, cultural institutions should carefully look at the needs of their visitors and the resources and requirements of their organization. Technology initiatives should be undertaken because they are beneficial and not simply be technology for the sake of technology.

When investigating the use of mobile technology for special collections, the following guidelines may prove useful:

1. *Determine what collections would be of greatest interest to your visitors.* Mobile smartphones are used in a different manner from desktop web applications. Frequently, the mobile user is concerned with material that is related to their current geographic location. Among the many collections held by an institution, there are likely some that are more useful to view via mobile technology or to which users would like more immediate access.

2. *Use collections that have already been digitized.* Digitization projects can be lengthy and consume many resources. If the mobile technology project makes use of existing digitized resources, the development time for the project should decrease substantially.

3. *Take advantages of partnerships with other institutions.* Many organizations may not have the resources to create their own mobile technology projects. Working with other institutions in a formal or informal partnership can help share the burden of technical development time and costs. Some organizations may already have mobile technology projects to which another institution's collections could be added.

4. *Use existing applications.* If an existing digital catalog has an application programming interface option, it may be possible to build a new mobile app by leveraging existing collection management database services. Organizations that cannot build their own application or take advantage of partnerships may also be able to use existing commercial services to display their collections. Several photo sharing sites, such as Flickr, Picasa, and Snapfish, have mobile versions that enable users to view photos using their mobile phones. Although placing images on a photo sharing site may raise copyright and branding concerns, it also provides an affordable and low-maintenance opportunity to introduce audiences to the collections via mobile technology.

5. *Investigate the best technology for your collection.* Mobile technology can mean many things. One organization may develop a walking tour that accesses materials from a local history collection, whereas another institution may make digitized versions of their maps available for online download. Some projects can be built by an internal technology staff member, whereas others will require the assistance of a technology or design company. Institutions should research possible options for mobile technology before committing to a specific project.

6. *Get the public involved.* Increasing public access is a prominent goal of many mobile technology projects. To ensure that the final application will be regularly used, encourage public feedback throughout the design process. An institution's visitors can provide valuable insight into an application's user interface and overall structure. By integrating users into

the development process, a library can also begin building an audience for the application at a very early stage.

ENHANCING THE USER EXPERIENCE: FUTURE PLANS FOR MOBILE TECHNOLOGY

On February 1, 2010, the National Endowment for the Humanities awarded the City of Philadelphia, Department of Records a Digital Humanities Start-Up Grant to support the development of a mobile phone application that would use augmented reality technology. For this project, augmented reality technology refers to the overlay of digital data on a live view of the physical world via the camera embedded in contemporary smartphones. The DOR plans to create an application that will enable users to view overlays of historic photographs on live camera images of the current landscape using their smartphones.[7] Initial plans are to make overlays available for 500 photographs and provide additional contextual information for 20 of those images.

Digital Humanities Start-Up grants are "designed to encourage innovations in the digital humanities."[8] Although some work on augmented reality and historic photo collections has been completed by the Museum of London[9] and the Powerhouse Museum in Sydney, Australia,[10] the DOR hopes to use this grant to further investigate the use of augmented reality as an educational tool for archival and special collections. Once the prototype is completed in spring 2011, the project team plans to release a whitepaper detailing their findings for use by other cultural institutions investigating augmented reality applications.

In addition to augmented reality technology, other features could increase access to the collections via mobile applications. Although the smartphone app enables the public to view images throughout Philadelphia, users currently cannot contribute their own content. A possible extension of the current platform would be a feature that accepts public submissions. Perhaps an individual at the location where a historic image was originally taken could snap a photo using their cell phone or send a text message with their thoughts about the image or landscape. This content could then be added to the database to encourage additional comments about the images and contribute to the overall history of the location. Supporting audio or video content for download would also assist with providing further information about the cultural institution and its collections.

Adding features or developing options for public participation creates new challenges, as well as exciting opportunities. Although user-generated content requires administrative management and raises copyright concerns, it also provides an opportunity for libraries and other organizations to connect with their users and create a truly collaborative experience around special collections.

CONCLUSION

Since its launch in 2005, *Philly*History.org has grown to be a vital part of the historic community in Philadelphia. In addition to meeting the goals of organizing the images, preserving them physically and digitally, increasing public access, and generating revenue, the web site has also become a collaborative tool and encourages the public to connect with the collections. With the addition of the mobile application, *Philly*History.org reached new audiences and confirmed its commitment to using mobile technology to truly connect the past with the present in Philadelphia. The augmented reality application hopefully to be released in early 2011 will continue to foster and reinforce the idea that neglected collections can have another life rooted in the contemporary world. With 6,000 registered users, more than $60,000 in revenue from print sales and license requests, and images from five cultural institutions, *Philly*History.org serves as an example of how a regional consortium of collections can successfully operate together. It also demonstrates how mobile technology initiatives can serve as a valuable tool for libraries and other institutions to promote and display their special collections.

NOTES

1. Dolores Hayden, *The Power of Place: Urban Landscapes as Public History* (Cambridge, MA: MIT Press, 1997), 46.

2. "WolfWalk," NCSU Libraries, accessed August 31, 2010, http://www.lib.ncsu.edu/wolfwalk/.

3. Sean Aery, June 16, 2009, "Library Digital Collections? There's an App for That," *Duke University Libraries Digital Collections Blog*, accessed August 31, 2010, http://library.duke.edu/blogs/digital-collections/2009/06/16/library-digital-collections-theres-an-app-for-that/.

4. Antone Gonsalves, "Android Phone Steals Market Share," *InformationWeek*, April 7, 2010, accessed May 28, 2010, http://www.informationweek.com/news/mobility/smart_phones/showArticle.jhtml?articleID=224201745.

5. Amanda Lenhart, Rich Ling, Scott Campbell, and Kristen Purcell, "Teens and Mobile Phones," Pew Internet & American Life Project, April 20, 2010, accessed May 25, 2010, http://www.pewinternet.org/Reports/2010/Teens-and-Mobile-Phones.aspx.

6. David Ferriero, April 27, 2010, "The Future is in the Palm of Our Hands," *AOTUS: Collector in Chief*, accessed, May 28, 2010, http://blogs.archives.gov/aotus/?p=236.

7. "Historic Overlays on Smart Phones," National Endowment for the Humanities Office of Digital Humanities, accessed August 31, 2010, http://www.neh.gov/ODH/Default.aspx?tabid=111&id=152.

8. "National Endowment for the Humanities Digital Humanities Start-Up Grants," National Endowment for the Humanities, accessed May 25, 2010, http://www.neh.gov/grants/guidelines/digitalhumanitiesstartup.html.

9. "Streetmuseum," Museum of London, accessed August 28, 2010, http://www.museumoflondon.org.uk/MuseumOfLondon/Resources/app/you-are-here-app/index.html.

10. Seb Chan, April 16, 2010, "New version of Powerhouse Museum in Layar: Augmented Reality Browsing of Museum Photos around Sydney," *Fresh + New(er)*, accessed May 25, 2010, http://www.powerhousemuseum.com/dmsblog/index.php/2010/04/16/new-version-of-powerhouse-museum-in-layar-augmented-reality-browsing-of-museum-photos-around-sydney/.

Mobile Use in Medicine: Taking a Cue from Specialized Resources and Devices

BOHYUN KIM

Florida International University Medical Library, Miami, FL

MARISSA BALL

Florida International University Green Library, Miami, FL

This article compares mobile resources and the use of mobile devices in medicine and healthcare with those in non-practice-based disciplines, examines libraries' challenges in providing access to mobile resources, and explores the questions of whether and how mobile devices will be able to offer unique benefits to students, instructors, and researchers as mobile technologies continue to advance. This article is based on the presentation, "Mobile Access to Licensed Databases in Medicine and Other Subject Areas," given at the Handheld Librarian Online Conference II on February 17, 2010.

INTRODUCTION

In an effort to serve an increasingly mobile patron population, libraries are now acquiring and creating more mobile-device-friendly content and developing new services. However, library content, particularly electronic databases and e-journals, has been lacking in providing proper interfaces or applications optimized for a mobile. Although some major subscription database vendors have recently begun to address this issue, today's mobile resources and the use of mobile devices for pedagogical or research purposes are, overall, in a very early stage of development. By contrast, in medicine and healthcare, mobile devices were introduced much earlier than in other disciplines and have been widely adopted for both medical education and clinical practice. Mobile devices are also closely integrated into the day-to-day activities of medical students, trainees, and practitioners.

Why are mobile resources and devices popular and widely used in medicine and healthcare disciplines, while in other disciplines, they only receive limited use as a tool for teaching, learning, and research activities in other disciplines? Will mobile devices become popular in non-practice-based disciplines, as they did in medicine? If so, what types of uses would they be put to? The answer to these questions can be found by comparing the different contexts in which mobile resources are used in medicine and other non-practice-based disciplines, and by considering the potential use of mobile devices for teaching, learning, and research that is not applicable to non-mobile devices.

HANDHELD USERS, EXCPECTATIONS, AND CURRENT PRACTICE

Data regarding the current mobile landscape tells us that "62 percent of all Americans . . . have either used a cell phone or PDA for a non-voice data application or logged on to the internet away from home or work using a wireless laptop connection or with a handheld device" (Horrigan 2008, 1). In addition, more than 54 million smartphones were shipped in the first quarter of 2010 in the United States, a marked increase of 49% compared to the same period in 2009; a similar 2010 projection estimates that 1.3 billion mobile phones will ship worldwide, with 250 million of them being smartphones (Whitney 2010). Simple cell phones no longer rule the mobile market, and consumers are trending toward gadgets and technologies that offer advanced capabilities and multiple functions such as the iPhone, iPad, iPod Touch, Android, netbook, laptop and personal digital assistants (PDAs), moving away from devices that have a single dedicated purpose. Technological advances have also led to the physical size of computers getting smaller while their capacities and functionalities are growing and expanding exponentially. Increasingly, we see the boundaries between handheld devices and desktops blurring. Consumer practice is propelling the demand for both mobile devices and sophisticated mobile capabilities.

These mobile consumers are also our library users. Therefore, one can also presume that they would expect similarly advanced mobile capabilities and functions in association with their information and learning resources/services. These new handheld workstations are a part of our users' everyday lives and, correspondingly, handheld as a platform for delivering and receiving information has become an expectation. This perfect storm of rapid technological advances and ever-present devices equals a willing and engrossed end user. To libraries, these potentials and opportunities would seem an idyllic state of affairs. However, we are faced with certain realities and practices regarding our users, information providers, and services that are postponing progress. In reality, mobile browsing capabilities exist only on approximately 60% of handsets today; although that number is expected to increase to more than 80% in 2013 (Shen et al. 2009), it may presently be a basis for the infancy of mobile development in the library world.

The adoption and implementation of mobile technology by libraries has taken a variety of forms: mobile-friendly library websites or add-ons to institutional mobile applications and sites, finding aids, mobile catalogs, and actual service via short message service (SMS)-enabled chat. These portable library platforms reformat basic information about collections or services for the mobile medium and relay it in a quickly and easily digestible manner. But the role of mobile technology in these platforms remains supplementary. Little consideration is given to the learning and research aspect of mobile library services. In a future where the Pew Internet and American Life Project predicts that mobile devices will be the primary Internet connection tools for most people in the world by 2020 (Rainie and Anderson 2008), libraries and their information providers have a lot of catching up to do.

HANDHELD PUZZLE: FINDING THE RIGHT FIT

When looking at the broad range of research tools and resources available to a library user on a traditional desktop computer, one would expect comparable conveniences to be available for mobile platforms. However, licensed resources do not offer these same options. General and interdisciplinary resources are almost nonexistent for a mobile device, with the exception of EBSCO's relatively small selection of EBSCOhost Mobile Interface databases and Gale's AccessMyLibrary. The rest of the research resources available are comprised of tools and platforms created for a small number of niche, subject-specific users and markets (Table 1). This "niche-domination" in mobile resource development is prominently exemplified in LexisNexis releasing mobile apps for its GetCases and Shepardize products rather than one for its well-known LexisNexis Academic database. Furthermore, Table 1 shows that current mobile resources from information providers do not yet support a broad variety of mobile operating systems.

Content providers are targeting mobile consumers directly as individual users and their primary customers rather than institutions and libraries. As a result, mobile versions of library databases and licensed content are often not available for institutional accounts. Licensed mobile resources also feature a varying degree of authentication processes (or no authentication at all as shown in Gale's AccessMyLibrary apps), varying location-awareness capability, limited search functionalities and search results within the resources, varying institutional branding options, varying availability between app and

TABLE 1 Niche-Domination in Licensed Mobile Resources

EBSCOhost mobile platform (includes most of EBSCO's databases)	Web-Based platform
Gale AccessMyLibrary	app [iPad, iPhone, or iPod-Touch]
IEEExplore	web-based platform
Naxos Music Library [NML, NML:Jazz]	app [iPad, iPhone, or iPod-Touch]
WestLaw	web-based platform
LexisNexis [GetCases & Shepardize]	app [iPad, iPhone, or iPod-Touch]
Hoover's	app [iPad, iPhone, or iPod-Touch]
American Institute of Physics iResearch	app [iPad, iPhone, or iPod-Touch]
Nature.com Mobile	app [iPad, iPhone, or iPod-Touch]
American Chemical Society	app [iPad, iPhone, or iPod-Touch]
Serials Solutions SummonsMobile	web-based platform
Alexander Street Press Music Online	app [iPad, iPhone, or iPod-Touch]
Others: WorldCat Mobile, Britannica Mobile	app [iPad, iPhone, or iPod-Touch], or web-based platform

mobile web site (Table 1), and varying associations with existing user desktop/web accounts. These varied, yet limited customization and settings options for the existing mobile applications and platforms further underscore the impression of the individual user as a target customer/consumer rather than institutions and libraries; the library as a customer has been left behind. It soon becomes apparent that our handheld adopters, the on-demand and on-the-go "mobile-centrics" (Horrigan 2007), are driving the bus. Their habits, lifestyles, and behaviors are influencing how and what is being developed. Information providers and research tool developers are looking at trends that are emerging outside of the library world for ideas of future development—as should libraries.

Where information providers are finding niche markets and subject areas with established user-bases to develop content for, libraries are on a divergent path, casting a wider and generalized net yet catching less. The reason for the slow mobile adoption at libraries is not so much a lack of technology or desire as lack of understanding of their fit in the puzzle of mobile integration with teaching, learning, and service. Traditional research and learning techniques do not easily translate into the mobile platform, and sometimes they conflict with each other. Research in non-practice-based disciplines often employs more comprehensive and exhaustive information gathering and processing methods that are not yet quite portable. When "mobile learning is about how effectively and quickly you can search for and retrieve the information you need" (Johnson, Levine, Smith, and Stone 2010), a platform or app that retrieves overly limiting search results and offers inadequate search capabilities becomes a burdensome and onerous learning and research tool. Therefore, in looking at how mobile devices are being used in a more specialized sphere and following the trends of the early developers among the information providers, one can begin to generate ideas for future mobile developments for libraries.

THE USE OF MOBILE DEVICES AND RESOURCES IN MEDICINE AND HEALTHCARE

The number of mobile device users in medicine and healthcare is significantly higher than in other disciplines. Fifty-four percent of U.S. doctors own a PDA< or a smartphone, and more than half of them consider it an integral part of their practice (iHealthBeat 2009). Among students and trainees, mobile device use is even higher; 60% to 70% of medical students and residents use handheld devices for education or patient care (Kyo, Henderson, Dressler, and Kripalani 2006).

What is notable regarding mobile device use in medicine and healthcare is the extent to which it is embedded into clinical practice and medical education. At the point of care, mobile devices are used for both clinical decision support and workplace learning. Mobile devices allow doctors, nurses, and other healthcare professionals to immediately access reference, procedural, and research evidence information wherever they are. In addition, mobile devices are capable of pushing out alerts and reminders about news and research information relevant to users' specific clinical interest, thereby facilitating continuing education and workplace learning (Doran 2009). Mobile devices are also used for healthcare communication and accessing patient records making medical practice more efficient.

Mobile devices are also increasingly being used in medical education. Many medical schools provide lecture content as a video or a podcast for later study, and, in turn, students use their mobile devices to watch or listen to those lecture videos or podcasts (Ducut and Fontelo 2008). Instructors rely on mobile devices to collect immediate results from polls and evaluation surveys. Medical students also use anatomical diagrams, medical calculators, and study guides on their mobile devices and consider their mobile devices as "mobile libraries" that carry medical information wherever they go in clinical settings (Ducut and Fontelo 2008). For this reason, some medical schools require that their students purchase handheld devices during their clinical years.

Due to the early adoption and popularity of mobile devices in medicine, medical and health sciences libraries have been on the vanguard in providing access to mobile resources to handheld users among their patrons. Those resources include licensed databases, free resources, guides for choosing mobile resources, instructions about how to set up certain mobile resources on a specific type of mobile devices, and mobile versions of library web sites. Some medical libraries also loan mobile devices with specific resources preinstalled, provide support for software installation and updates for users' mobile devices, and hold user-training sessions on using mobile devices and resources.

As pioneers in providing support and services for mobile device users, medical and health sciences libraries have encountered many challenges. Non-medical libraries are likely to face similar challenges as they begin to reach out to the increasing number of mobile device users among their patrons. First, it is difficult for a library to gauge actual demand for mobile resources. To develop a useful mobile resources collection, a library needs to know not only the number of library users who own a mobile device, but also how many of them actually use a mobile device to access mobile resources. The fact that mobile resource vendors do not offer much in the way of usage statistics only adds to the challenge. Although mobile resource vendors typically require each user to create a personal account and to report what type of a device they own, the gathered information, the actual usage amount, and the usage patterns are rarely made available to libraries.

Second, libraries have to deal with many different licensing models. Koufogiannakis, Ryan, and Dahl (2005) and Cuddy and Wrynn (2007) both provide detailed information about a variety of licensing models for mobile electronic resources and the advantages and disadvantages of each model: free with existing licensed product, user add-on purchase, institutional site license, set number of downloads, electronic loaning with due dates, and freeware. Mobile resources can also be made accessible through mobile devices that already have those resources preinstalled, as shown in the case of the American Association of Critical-Care Nurses' PDA and Mobile Resources Center (American Association of Critical-Care Nurses 2008). A library has to carefully choose resources among varying licensing models and determine which are suitable for the local users' needs and preferences, as well as for the library's available funding.

Third, libraries need to make an extra effort in marketing their mobile resources and educating users about the different versions of licensed resources. Traditionally, mobile resources are used primarily as personal organization tools. For this reason, mobile device users may not understand the potential academic or pedagogical use of a mobile device (Fischer et al. 2003). Furthermore, the personal nature of a mobile device often leads information providers to directly marketing their mobile products directly to individual users rather than to libraries. As a result, users who are unaware of the availability of a mobile resource through a library may purchase the identical mobile resource at their own expense. For marketing purposes, vendors also advertise a free (often-called "lite") version of a mobile resource with limited content and functionalities, which bears the same name as the paid version. Unknowingly, users may use a lite version even when the paid version with full content and functionalities is available through the library.

Fourth, libraries need to provide additional support for users who access licensed databases through the required registration, authentication, download, and installation process. Many mobile resources are available only on certain mobile platforms. Users may need help in identifying resources that not only meet their needs, but also support the specific type of mobile device that they own. Although some of the higher-end smart-phones now make it relatively easy to download and install various mobile applications, the set-up process of downloading PDA software on a desk-top computer and synching it with PDA devices can be daunting for many non-tech-savvy users.

Almost all licensed resources require a user to follow certain steps for registration, authentication, download, and installation. For example, the mobile versions of Dynamed and Natural Standard for the iPhone and iPod Touch device require the download and installation of a free application called Skyscape. The users who want to download the mobile version of Dynamed are also required to request a serial number through a library, which automatically expires at the end of the year. Similarly, while mobile resources in the form of a mobile web site rather than a stand-alone application should be simpler to access, they also have certain restrictions. For example, the mobile version of MD Consult prohibits a user from using more than one type of device at a time. If a user has previously logged in to the web version of MD Consult, he or she cannot simultaneously access the mobile version. All of these small and large restrictions and requirements may frustrate library users who try to access the library's mobile resources. To minimize such frustrations, libraries will need to be proactive in informing users about possible issues and helping them to overcome various technical barriers.

Lastly, as shown in the difficulties and challenges noted above, making mobile resources accessible to library users requires additional funding and investment in staff time. To evaluate mobile resources and provide support for their download, installation, and access, a library may have to purchase a mobile device for testing and training purposes. The library staff also has to be trained about how to use different types of mobile devices and how to install and access the library's mobile resources on those devices. To reduce the burden of supporting mobile device users, libraries can seek partnerships with other units, such as an information technology department within their organization.

A survey of 366 medical students from George Washington University and the University of Maryland conducted in 2004 showed that the most common area of dissatisfaction among medical students with handheld devices was the lack of institutional support (Grasso, Jim Yen, and Mintz 2006). This included concerns that handheld computers were not integrated with their hospital information systems, that each training location had different computer requirements, and that their medical schools were not committed to using handheld computers. Although library service was not part of the cited lack of institutional support, this survey result indicates that a library can play a key role in improving much-desired institutional support by providing relevant mobile resources and offering support and services for mobile device users.

FUTURE DIRECTIONS FOR MOBILE RESOURCES

In 2007, Spires surveyed 766 librarians (mostly from academic libraries) on their use and the perceived use of their customers of PDAs, smartphones, webpads, and other handheld wireless devices. The survey result showed that although some libraries, particularly those in medicine and health-care, had already begun to serve the mobile device users among library patrons, the majority of librarians were uncertain about the percentage of their patrons using mobile devices, how mobile devices were being used in their libraries, and whether there was a demand for more or different services for mobile device users (Spires 2008).

The survey result also showed that 19.4% of librarians among those surveyed owned a mobile device and that 69.2% of those librarians used their mobile devices as a personal organization tool for functions such as e-mail, calendar/scheduling, web browsing, contact/address book, and note taking. Interestingly, only 28.6% of those librarians used their mobile devices to access library content such as databases, e-journals, or e-books. Even among those librarians, however, the most-accessed content was the local library catalog. The surveyed librarians commented that mobile devices were ill-equipped to access the majority of library content, particularly subscribed resources, because of the small screen size, keyboard, memory, slow speed, and high device price and monthly fees.

However, many of these limitations have been greatly improved since the time of this survey in 2007. Today's higher-end smartphones enable users to browse the Internet without much difficulty with their faster processing speed, larger memory, and bigger touch screens equipped with zooming features. Considering that the largest growth in the mobile device market is seen in these higher-end smartphones (Whitney 2010), it is no surprise that mobile resource vendors are also mostly targeting higher-end smartphone users in developing mobile products. The release of the iPad in 2010 testified to the growing potential of a mobile device with capabilities that are almost equal to desktop computers.

However, the technological advancement in recent smartphones has still not yet reached the point to make mobile devices adopted as a common pedagogical and research tool in all academic disciplines. Unlike in practice-based disciplines, such as medicine, students, educators, and researchers, in other disciplines lack a compelling reason to use mobile resources for their day-to-day learning, teaching, and research activities. Their information needs are for in-depth study and research rather than for quick decision making and the guidance to immediate patient treatment.

Unlike medicine and healthcare trainees and professionals, students, instructors, and researchers in non-practice-based disciplines also have flexibility in the time-frame of their research and the work environment. As far as the traditional study and research process in non-practice-based disciplines is concerned, today's mobile device is still a supplementary tool as it is yet to be able to completely support their study, teaching, and research pattern and workflow. Even the iPad, the most recent and powerful mobile device, does not allow users to easily download files from the Internet and to transfer them between different applications or between itself and other mobile devices or desktop computers.

On the other hand, there are capabilities such as location-awareness, sensory data input, immediate audiovisual feedback to such input, and augmented reality, which only mobile devices can offer. As a mobile device further evolves, it may be able to establish itself as a common pedagogical, learning, and research tool in non practice-based disciplines. Some of the innovative uses of a mobile device tapping on these capabilities are already observed in medicine and healthcare (Mobile Monday Amsterdam 2010). For example, an application called Pocket CPR for iPhone and iPod Touch helps a medical trainee learn and perform the CPR procedure correctly by providing the immediate audio and video feedback of the trainee's performance. This application hints at the way in which a mobile device can play a unique role in students' learning. Another application called iStethoscope transforms an iPhone or an iPod Touch into a digital stethoscope that not only listens to but also measures and records a patient's heartrate and breathing sounds. This application also generates spectrograms from those recordings.

It is easy to think of other similar cases in which a mobile device can be used to collect and record sensory data for a research project in the field. For example, students and researchers in disciplines such as anthropology, biology, and environmental studies may be able to use a mobile device to collect research data when they are in the field. Using a mobile device for research data collection itself is not a new idea (Fischer et al. 2003). However, data collection by automatic detection and recording from the outside world rather than by manual input is an area that has not been explored much. In addition, the location-awareness feature of a mobile device combined with augmented reality applications will provide opportunities for instructors to improve their teaching practice and offer great learning experience to students who are visiting historic sites or cultural institutions such as a museum.

CONCLUSION

Many mobile resources for academic disciplines and the application of mobile devices to teaching, learning, and research tools, are still in the very early stages of development. Although mobile devices are simultaneously becoming more popular and powerful, their use at present is limited to quickly obtaining brief information on the go. Mobile devices are also regarded primarily as a personal organization tool, and for this reason, users may well be unfamiliar with their use for academic and research purposes. This explains why in disciplines that require access to quick information in the field such as medicine, both mobile devices and resources are widely used and relied on, whereas in other disciplines, they are still being regarded as a secondary and supplementary tools.

It is too soon to tell what pedagogical roles a mobile device will play in the future. However, one thing is certain: as mobile technologies rapidly advance, the traditional method of teaching, learning, and research will inevitably undergo changes to take advantage of those technologies. Accordingly, a handheld device will accordingly find its niche where mobile technologies, data, and resources intersect to meet the particular needs of users engaged in specific teaching, learning, and research activities. Libraries will benefit from studying mobile device users' behavior and the usage patterns of mobile resources. This will help libraries develop services that support users' actual tasks and workflows and deliver library content in a way that directly supports those tasks and workflows.

REFERENCES

American Association of Critical-Care Nurses. 2008. "AACN's PDA and Mobile Resources Center." Accessed May 23, 2010. http://aacn.pdaorder.com/welcome.xml.

Cuddy, Colleen, and Paul Wrynn. 2007. "Licensing Content for PDAs." *Journal of Electronic Resources in Medical Libraries* 4: 175–84.

Doran, Diane. 2009. "The Emerging Role of PDAs in Information Use and Clinical Decision Making." *Evidence Based Nursing* 12: 35–8.

Ducut, Emily, and Paul Fontelo. 2008. "Mobile Devices in Health Education: Current Use and Practice." *Journal of Computing in Higher Education* 20(2): 59–68.

Fischer, Sandra, Thomas E. Stewart, Sangeeta Mehta, Randy Wax, and Stephen E. Lapinsky. 2003. "Handheld Computing in Medicine." *Journal of the American Medical Informatics Association* 10(2): 139–149.

Grasso, Michael, M. Jim Yen, and Matthew L. Mintz. 2006. "Survey of Handheld Computing among Medical Students." *Computer Methods and Programs in Medicine* 82: 196–202.

Horrigan, John. 2007. "A Typology of Information and Communication Technology Users." Pew Internet and American Life Project. Accessed January 2010. http://www.pewinternet.org/Reports/2007/A-Typology-of-Information-and-Communication-Technology-Users.aspx.

Horrigan, John. 2008. "Mobile Access to Data and Information." Pew Internet and American Life Project. Accessed January 2010. http://www.pewinternet.org/Reports/2008/Mobile-Access-to-Data-and-Information.aspx.

iHealthBeat. 2009. "Smartphones Becoming Integral Tools for Health Care Providers, Medical Students." Accessed May 23, 2010. http://www.ihealthbeat. org/Special-Reports/2009/Smartphones-Becoming-Integral-Tools-for-Health-Care-Providers-Medical-Students.aspx.

Johnson, L., A. Levine, R. Smith, and S. Stone. 2010. "The 2010 Horizon Report." *The New Media Consortium.* Accessed February 2010. http://wp.nmc.org/horizon2010/.

Koufogiannakis, Denise, Pam Ryan, and Susan Dahl. 2005. "Just Another Format: Integrating Resources for Users of Personal Digital Assistants." *The Acquisitions Librarian* 17: 133–45.

Kyo, Anna, Laura E. Henderson, Daniel D. Dressler, and Sunil Kripalani. 2006. "Use of Handheld Computers in Medical Education: A Systematic Review." *Journal of General Internal Medicine* 21: 531–7.

Mobile Monday Amsterdam. 2010. "Ivor Ković - An EMR Physician with an iPhone." Accessed February 2, 2010. http://www.youtube.com/watch?v=Q-EB3Pc8mk&feature=player_embedded.

Rainie, L., and J. Anderson. 2008. "The Future of the Internet III." Pew Internet and American Life Project. Accessed February 2, 2010. http://www.pewinternet.org/Reports/2008/The-Future-of-the-Internet-III.aspx.

Shen, S., T. J. Hart, N. Ingelbrecht, A. Zimmermann, J. Ekholm, N. Jones, J. Edwards, and A. Frank. 2009. "Gartner Identifies the Top 10 Consumer Mobile Applications for 2012." Gartner Newsroom. Accessed February 25, 2010. http://www.gartner.com/it/page.jsp?id=1230413.

Spires, Todd. 2008. "Handheld Librarians: A Survey of Librarian and Library Patron Use of Wireless Handheld Devices." *Internet Reference Services Quarterly* 13: 287–309.

Whitney, Lance. 2010. "Cell Phone, Smartphone Sales Surge." *CNet News*, May 19, 2010. Accessed May 23, 2010. http://news.cnet.com/8301-1035_3-20005359-94.html.

Tag, You're It! Using QR Codes to Promote Library Services

BEATRICE PULLIAM and CHRIS LANDRY
Providence College, Providence, RI

The authors discuss how Quick Response code technology can be used to market library services innovatively by introducing them in a more flexible way. The authors also provide real life examples of mobile tagging efforts underway, discuss best practices, and suggest possible implications of Quick Response use in libraries.

INTRODUCTION

According to many recent surveys on current technology trends, libraries and library services remain out of sync with user expectations. With ever-expanding digital resources, libraries must try to increase awareness of these new services and collections while making sure old formats are not being left behind. Many emerging technologies can be used to deliver and market library services.

One of the more interesting developments on the mobile front has been the trend of mobile tagging. For those who are not familiar with it, mobile tagging is a process that allows users to access digital content on their mobile device via an encoded object. If that seems a bit impenetrable, here is a familiar parallel: a book is being checked out to a patron. A laser reads the book's barcode and relays the information to a computer program. The computer program then reads that information to identify the book and perform the action of checking out. Similarly, a mobile tag provides information and suggests an action to an enabled mobile device. The big difference is that mobile devices can do way cooler things than an Integrated Library System.

For this communication to happen, you just need a few things: a mobile device with a camera, a program that can read the information, and the encoded object. (An Internet connection is only needed if the content is hosted online.) Although some services can encode an actual photographic image with information, the technology is relatively new and not widespread. More commonly, the encoding of an object is done through an intermediary such a two-dimensional barcode, also known as a matrix code. Matrix codes can contain loads of data, because they are stored in a non-linear fashion, hence the "2D" label. This opens up the possibility for a vast range of designs—some better than others. Of the many developed, the one we will be focusing on is the Quick Response (QR) code.

QR codes were developed by the Japanese corporation Denso Wave (http://www.denso-wave.com/en/index.html) in 1996. Since their introduction, QR codes (Figure 1) have become absolutely pervasive throughout Japanese marketing. Several factors are responsible for their popularity:

- QR is dynamic—Let's say you have a QR code that prompts a mobile device to open a page on your library's web site. If the URL ever changes, you can revise the underlying data without having to alter the code's image.
- QR is freely available—A lot of free online QR generators exist, and Denso Wave chooses not to exercise its patent rights. Most generators offer free scanning software for users.
- QR is an ISO (International Organization for Standardization) standard—No matter what region they are created in, a QR code is going to be a QR code.
- QR is well-designed—With a higher capacity than other matrix codes, such as Data Matrix, QR is an ideal container for large amounts of data. QR also sports great size variability and error correction capabilities. Up to 30% of damaged or obscured data can be restored.
- QR is enriching—QR codes tie the physical to the digital. They also can deliver content with a great depth of interactivity.

WHY QR?

Nationally, Internet trend scouts, such as The Pew Internet & American Life Project, have reported that approximately 85% of American adults (those 18 years and older) own handheld devices (Horrigan 2009). More locally, we also noticed that many more of our students were using handheld devices (smartphones or cell phones) in their daily activities on campus and have recently seen an uptick in requests for assistance connecting iPhones to our wireless network. These factors, combined with a less than robust web site

FIGURE 1 QR Code which leads to an instructional Libguide on QR codes.

and a need to market our content and services in a new way, eventually led us to investigate the use of QR codes.

So often, many new initiatives at the Providence College Library have arisen out of informal "show and tell" tech conversations that happen among the staff. A casual curiosity with augmented reality and gadgets exposed a bit of potential in the use of QR technology within libraries. QR was a flexible tool that was free and easy to use. It was also a timely discovery as we had just begun several other mobile initiatives.

To start, we set our focus on QR itself. If we were going to use these codes, we needed to know what they were beneath the surface. It is not necessary to know every little detail, but a good grasp on the nitty-gritty will help avoid problems. Doing a simple Google search for "QR code" will bring up plenty of technical information. The English version of the Denso Wave web site (http://www.denso-wave.com/qrcode/index-e.html) has a fairly detailed overview that proved useful. Once we were familiar with QR codes, our focus shifted to the important question: who can use it?

SELECT YOUR TECH

It is usually good practice to poll your user-base before starting a project that involves emerging technologies. Well, we actually did not in this case.

The investment for this project was low enough: just staff time and personal cell phones to begin. In house, we had an Apple iPhone, two Android-based phones, and two BlackBerry devices. This small variety provided us with a pretty decent idea of platform compatibility. (However, it would have been nice to test programs out on the Nokia Symbian OS too.) As most free QR scanning programs are cross-platform, we had no trouble finding some to test. It then was just a matter of figuring out which programs would meet our users' needs.

Preliminary research whittled down the options quickly. We ultimately did extensive testing with the Beetagg (http://www.beetagg.com/) and ScanLife (http://www.scanlife.com/us/) scanning programs. Although our decision hinged mostly on their price (both are free), their reliability, and the ease of use, the fact that both companies offered online generators and management services certainly came into play. For that side of the equation, we ended up using the Beetagg Manager. It is simple, provides statistics, and is 100% free. Keep in mind though that what worked for us may not be ideal for others, so we highly recommend taking time to do the research before settling on one service. It even took us additional testing to figure out which of the two services could best mesh with our production standards. Once all the elements involved were set out, it was time to present it to "a higher power," namely, our library director.

GETTING BUY-IN

Library administration at Providence College has been very supportive of the use of emerging technologies in delivery of library content and services. We approached our library director about piloting QR codes in conjunction with the rollout of our "Take Your Library for a Walk" initiative, our new suite of mobile services that includes a mobile library info site (http://m.providence.edu/library), EBSCOHost Mobile database search, and our new Short Messaging Service (SMS) reference service. Our library director also helped us test the traction of QR codes by wearing a library staff-designed QR code tee shirt during his presentation at the 2010 American Library Association (ALA) Midwinter Meeting in Boston. When scanned, the QR code directs you to the director's articles available through Providence College's Digital Commons, our institutional repository. Staff and community awareness are also very important, so we also created a LibGuide (http://providence.libguides.com/qr) that provides descriptive information about QR codes and related terminology. The LibGuide also has useful information on QR reader selection and the library's QR code projects to date.

Uses of QR

As with many new technologies, implementations tend to vary across environments. Some more popular uses include promotion of products, events and services, the use of QR codes to build local online communities (i.e., Google's Favorite Places Project http://www.google.com/help/maps/favoriteplaces/gallery/), and the incorporation of QR code as an interactive design element. Some of the best examples of QR in play can be found in the Flickr Group Pool QR in the Wild (http://www.flickr.com/groups/qrcodes/), which has captured more than 600 examples of QR codes in use around the world in the past year.

QR IN LIBRARIES

Some uses for QR codes in libraries (public, academic, and special/museum) that we think will have some traction include using QR codes to:

1. Promote library events/special collections.
2. Make services more discoverable.
3. Create digital "wayfinders" in the stacks.

Dover Public Library in Dover, Massachusetts, for example, set up a QR station to create awareness about the use of QR codes within the library and integrated QR codes into a kid's summer reading and activity program. In the academic arena, both the University of Bath and University of Huddersfield in the United Kingdom added QR codes to records in their library catalogs. Many instances of QR codes as a digital supplement to museum and special collections exhibits may also be found around the Internet.

Our own initial use of QR at the Providence College Library was in October 2009. A QR code was included in promotional materials for a Banned Books Week discussion. When scanned, the QR code took the user to ALA's Banned Books web site. We included it so see whether it would generate any curiosity. It did not attract much attention, only five "clicks" (QR scans in Beetagg speak) to date, at least two-thirds of which were probably from our own testing. Later, we created the QR LibGuide mentioned earlier, a functional QR code model made entirely of thumbtacks that was displayed in the lobby of the library and began more widespread integration of QR codes in promotional tools used to market some of our new mobile services. Our more recent attempts using QR codes have been more fruitful.

METRICS

Beetagg Manager, Beetagg's built-in statistics tool, has been very helpful to us for tracking scans of the QR codes. Statistics are kept online for each individual QR code, and Beetagg provides the total number of scans in both text and graphical (month-by-month) form. At 87, the QR Code LibGuide has the highest number of scans, followed by 27 for the Library Director's QR code, and 18 for the code created for a recent Special Collections exhibit. Most of our QR codes are linked to a shortened URL via bit.ly (a popular and free URL shortener and tracker (http://bit.ly), which has allowed for more granular statistics. We have not analyzed the data gathered too closely but have identified this as an important next step before moving to heavier QR code use.

SUCCESSES AND DRAWBACKS

An initiative like this can make your content and services more discoverable. It also opens up the possibility for your local community to be an online community. In addition, it places the library in the position of a tech leader. One concern though is keeping pace with your user-base. We may be ahead of their interests and, not to mention, their technology. QR scanning programs are not preinstalled on most American mobile devices. It is easy to download them, but this still may impede some potential users. Another issue is that the content being accessed may not be optimized for mobile devices. Prior to publishing anything with a QR code, view the content and see if there are any formatting issues. Likewise, consider the necessity of your codes. It can be tempting to use them for every project, but their impact can be lost if they are blanketing your library.

LOOKING AHEAD

With many projects, a good method reveals itself only through observation and experimentation. It then is just a matter of being adaptable to the situation. This is something we are keeping in mind as we expand our QR code initiative. We may find it necessary to have a clearer picture of our user-base and their interests. Several upcoming efforts could rely on that. We hope to start incentive-based marketing campaigns, such as contests, to add a further element of interactivity. Eventually, we would like to associate QR codes with Library of Congress subject headings so that patrons may access subject guides or related content while browsing the stacks. Many ideas for further uses of QR codes came up in open discussion during our presentation at the Handheld Librarian II online conference held in February

2010. These included connecting media to promotional items, geocaching, interactive environments (i.e., potential use in mobile giving/gaming), and digital or interactive tours.

CONCLUSION

What began as an experiment to change the way we deliver content and market our services has challenged us to reconsider the way we interact with our community. In this regard, we feel that we have already had some level of success and look forward to offering what we have learned to other libraries exploring this technology.

REFERENCE

Horrigan, John. 2009. "Online Access in a Multiplatform World." Pew Internet & American Life Project. Accessed February 10, 2010. http://www.pewinternet. org/Reports/2009/12-Wireless-Internet-Use/2-Online-access-in-a-multiplatform-world/2-A-portrait-of-access-and-wireless-use.aspx?r=1.

Are You Ready for E-readers?

ANNE BEHLER

Library Learning Services, Penn State University Libraries, University Park, PA

BINKY LUSH

Department For Information Technologies, Penn State University Libraries, University Park, PA

The Penn State University Libraries partnered with Sony Electronics, Inc., to test the Sony Reader in the academic environment. Since 2008, they have tested the Reader extensively in teaching, lending, and disability services. This article discusses the preliminary research project. Although not scientific in nature, the article presents findings from surveys of 239 participants in the classroom setting, 15 library users who borrowed Sony Readers, and a single participant and the director of the disability services portion of the project.

INTRODUCTION

Since late 2007, when Amazon released the first Kindle, e-readers and e-books have climbed to the forefront of public attention. In an age of multiplying digital content, these devices certainly made waves in the academic environment as well. In particular, many academic libraries have since begun pilot projects using a variety of different reader devices to investigate the possibilities for simplifying and innovating the content and related services they offer to users in light of the technologies that are available. Countless libraries have experimented with offering lending programs for their devices.

Others are attempting to answer the question of whether libraries can maximize the capabilities of the technology that people are using to better package and deliver the content that they offer. Some academic programs are launching in-classroom pilot projects that ask students to directly test the capabilities of the devices as related to their own needs. Many libraries have undertaken these initiatives on their own, whereas others have partnered with either Sony Electronics, Inc., or Amazon to design and carry out their projects. The project that the Penn State University Libraries have undertaken in partnership with Sony combines many of these scenarios in a preliminary, non-scientific study, testing Sony Readers in library lending, academic classrooms, and some specific disabilities services use cases. In all, 256 people have participated in the study.

PENN STATE CASE STUDY

Setting

The Penn State University Libraries at University Park serve as a hub for the libraries at all 24 of the university's campuses. The University Park campus is home to approximately 45,000 students and more than 3,000 faculty of the University's total 87,000 students and approximately 6,000 faculty. As one of the top ten Association of Research Libraries institutions in the country, the University Libraries have a reputation for innovation, research, and a strong rapport with many of the University's colleges and academic programs. Situated at the academic crossroads of the University, the Libraries serve as the content provider and information experts for all disciplines and user populations at Penn State and are thus the ideal place to bring the Reader to the University community.

In March 2008, the Penn State University Libraries proposed a partnership to both Amazon and Sony to research the utility of e-books in a higher education environment. In response to the proposal, Sony donated 100 PRS-505 E-Book Readers to the Penn State University Libraries for use in a pilot project. Amazon declined partnership at the time but has since joined forces with several other universities to test their devices. The one-year pilot project proposed to investigate the following four issues: the utility of portable e-books in a research library collection; the effect of reading devices on teaching, learning and reading; the utility of such a reading device for individuals needing adaptive technologies; and the ways that the Libraries' licensed and locally created digital content may be repurposed for use on portable reading devices. A project team, composed of librarians and staff from technical and public services as well as faculty from the Penn State Department of English and the Libraries Associate Dean for Digital and Scholarly Communications, was formed to design and carry out the project.

Library Logistics

To mobilize the 100 Sony Readers in a variety of settings, the project team first had to tackle the technical aspects of the project including content loading, cataloging and circulation policies, and logistics.

Sony's Technical Model

Sony's technical model was designed specifically for the individual home-consumer market rather than the academic environment. Sony allows for a single computer to hold one Sony Reader Library that can share content with up to five Sony Readers. These Readers must be registered or associated with that one computer. Any content purchased through the Sony Reader store and managed in the Sony Reader Library can be downloaded to any or all of the five associated Readers. Because the Penn State University Libraries Sony project involved 100 Readers, the challenge was to find a way to efficiently load all 100 Readers with a variety of titles without the need for 20 individual computers (one computer per 5 readers).

The Virtual Machine Solution

To circumvent the 1 computer to 5 devices technology model, the team experimented with VM Ware Workstation software, which allowed creation of nine virtual machines on each of two dedicated copmuters. In this way, there were 20 separate machines to work with (18 virtual plus the 2 physical machines) enough for 100 Sony Readers. Each of the 20 machines had an individual IP address and an external internet connection. This setup allowed for one Sony content library and five associated Readers per machine—20 libraries for a total of 100 Readers. To economize on memory for each virtual machine and to eliminate data loss in the case of machine failure, the drives were mapped to space on one of the Libraries' servers to hold purchased content. It was also necessary to have an individual e-mail account and password to log into each library for purchasing and loading content. A single e-mail account with 20 aliases allowed all e-mail and receipts from each library to be forwarded to a single e-mail address, keeping paperwork in one location accessible by a single login and password.

Although the most recently released Sony readers are wireless, the content association model is still home-consumer driven and is not any more conducive to efficiently loading large quantities of content.

Circulation and Cataloging

To keep track of and catalog the Readers, each one was assigned a standardized name, which also served as the device's call number and as the title field

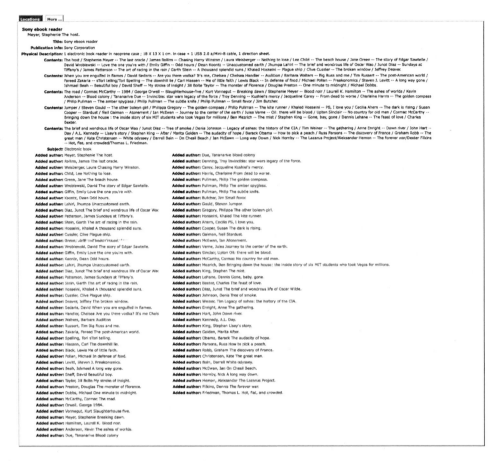

FIGURE 1 Catalog record for the sony reader.

in the cataloging record. All Readers were labeled and bar coded accordingly. The Readers, their basic operating instructions, and a USB cord were included together in a neoprene zipper pouch, with a "luggage tag" that included the Sony Reader name (call number) and the University Libraries' address.

The Readers were cataloged with the title Sony eBook Reader, the content listed in the 505 field of the MARC record, and the authors listed again in the 700 field (Figure 1). This allowed users to discover the readers by searching for the device itself or serendipitously by searching for a particular title or author's works.

SCENARIOS

Lending

In the Fall 2008 semester, the University Park campus made five Sony Readers available for lending to library users. Each of these Readers was populated with 10 titles of a particular theme or genre, including fiction and non-fiction bestsellers, science fiction and fantasy, books with film adaptations, and award-winning titles. The lending period for the readers was initially set to four weeks, with no ability for patrons to renew or place holds on the devices. Modeled after the library's existing laptop lending program, no signed contract was required to check out a Sony Reader. However, users were informed that they would be subject to a $25/day fine if the device was overdue, as well as the replacement cost should something happen or a Reader go missing. Each reader was checked out continuously through the semester to patrons who kept the devices for their entire four-week lending period.

Due to the program's popularity, the lending period for the Spring 2009 semester was shortened to two weeks so that more people would have an opportunity to try out the new service and assist in assessment. In addition, user feedback indicated that the theme of titles offered on the devices did not matter—they simply wanted variety in the titles available. In response, five additional Readers were added to the fleet, and titles were consolidated into one large preloaded library to maximize the content acquisitions. As a result of these changes, circulation of the Readers increased, as did the amount of feedback to the user experience survey. In addition, five Sony Readers are now being lent at Penn State Altoona, one of the University's 24 campuses, as part of this project. The project team anticipates learning much about the device's role in a smaller setting, where many of the students are commuters or non-traditional students.

CLASSROOMS

Libraries' First Year Seminar

The Libraries' First Year Seminar is designed to equip students with the tools necessary to navigate the vast world of information so that they can effectively assess, critique, and synthesize their discoveries through the research process. Throughout the class, students learn about the history of library and information sciences, principles of information storage, preservation and retrieval, research strategies and tools, and information ethics. These topics are reinforced through a variety of readings, as well as in-class and homework activities and discussion. Students are also asked to reflect on at least one important issue each week via blogs, a mode employed to encourage continued discourse outside of formal class sessions. The course culminates in group presentations that further explore at least one of the core concepts the class has discussed during the semester.

Because this course works to integrate analysis and use of information with a variety of different technologies, it provided an excellent laboratory for the use of e-book readers. In the Fall 2008 semester, this class employed the Sony Reader PRS-505 as the primary vehicle for required and optional texts and readings. All 18 students in the course opted to participate in the project and were issued a Sony Reader preloaded with the content for the course, as well as with several leisure reading titles that the students could peruse as they wished. In addition, students were encouraged to use the devices as carriers for other pertinent course documents—the instructors periodically sent PDF files to be uploaded to the devices—and to experiment with their application to other courses the students were taking.

English Department Classes

The English Honors Freshman Composition Course combines extensive writing experiences within the context of a complex and demanding reading list. Honors English, or English 30, is comprised of predominantly first-year students in the Humanities at an advanced reading level who read from multiple media sources per day. Forty-eight students in two sections of Honors English were volunteer participants in the study.

The Penn State University Libraries preloaded the Sony Readers for these students with the required texts for the class, all of which were titles purchased from the Sony Reader Store. The students were given a brief tutorial on the Sony Readers during one of their first class sessions and were expected to use the device for all of their reading assignments. Students were also asked to download additional content from course reserves or other online sources. Every three to four weeks, the students participated in video/audio-taped interviews and answered survey questions about their experiences with the Sony Reader. At the end of the semester, students presented their experiences and recommendations for the use of the devices as a learning tool to Sony representatives, faculty, and members of the Libraries Sony Project Team.

Sony Readers have also been used in an English graduate seminar, as well as with a class called Basic Writing Skills, designed for students who require remedial reading and writing instruction. Both of these classes followed much the same model as the English 30 classes, the primary difference being the class population and makeup.

Libraries' Office of Disability Services

The hope in using the Sony Readers in the Libraries Office of Services for Persons with Disabilities was that some of the functions of the Reader could assist patrons with limited vision or difficulties with dexterity.

Through this office, a student who was visually impaired had the opportunity to test a Reader. The student was asked to experiment with the various font sizes that the Sony Reader offers and to comment on the ability to easily navigate in and out of individual titles on the device given limited vision.

This person found that the type size did not increase sufficiently to allow for reading the text. In addition, the device was determined to be too difficult to navigate using memory or tactile skills without significant assistance from a seeing person. Similarly, patrons with dexterity difficulties found that the Reader was not any easier to use than traditional paper books. Navigating the Reader's content requires a high level of manual dexterity.

Despite the failure of this particular study, the director of the Libraries Office of Services for Persons with Disabilities is still very interested in eReading devices but would like to focus on readers designed specifically for people with disabilities. Of particular interest are those devices that will convert e-books or digitized text to speech. This functionality would assist patrons with limited vision, as well as those with learning difficulties. The Sony Reader currently does not have this functionality.

EVALUATION/FINDINGS

Lending

In addition to testing out the devices, patrons who borrowed a Sony Reader were invited to participate in a user experience survey following their time with the Sony Readers. Survey participants were asked the following questions:

1. Why did you check out a Sony Reader?
2. Which Sony Reader [theme/genre] did you check out? (question omitted in Spring)
3. What did you like about the Sony Reader?
4. What did you dislike about the Sony Reader?
5. Please list the books that you read from the Sony Reader.
6. Was the four-week (Spring: two-week) loan period long enough?
7. Did someone from the library staff show you how to use the Sony Reader?
8. Did you experience any problems with the Sony Reader?
9. If you did experience problems with the Sony Reader, please explain the problems.
10. Would you check out a Sony Reader from the library again?
11. Is there a title you would like to see made available on the Sony Reader?
12. How did you learn about the Sony Readers at the library?
13. Status [academic standing]:
14. Additional Comments:

In all, the survey received 15 responses. Although this number of responses is certainly not enough to draw any major conclusions, what follows is a summary of the salient findings. In response to the question, "Why did you check out a Sony Reader?," 13 of 15 users responded that they just wanted to try one of the devices. Other respondents noted they were motivated to use the Reader when they discovered a title in the library catalog that was otherwise not available. Four of five users also responded that the four-week loan period was enough time to have the Sony Reader. In the Spring, 9 of 10 users responded that two weeks was not enough time.

In terms of functionality and features, there were multiple mentions of the portability and content capacity as positive attributes. Battery life was mentioned favorably a handful of times, as was the ease of reading on the e-ink screen. Problems cited with the Sony Reader were the slow refresh time after page turns, glare on the screen, expense of purchasing, the desire for a backlight to ease strain on the eyes, and a small screen and text size. Although each Reader was loaded with several titles, the greatest number of titles any user noted reading was four. Only one person experienced technical difficulty in using the device, related to difficulty in charging the batteries. Several people offered extra comments, many recommending an on-demand title service or the ability to select titles other than those that were preloaded on the Readers.

Libraries' First Year Seminar

To gather data on the students' experiences, uses for the device, and impression of its functionality and application, students were asked to participate in user experience surveys. These surveys, administered at weeks 3, 6, and 10, asked the following questions of the participants:

1. What did you read on the Sony Reader?
2. When reading on the Sony, what else were you doing?
3. Where were you when you were reading on the Sony Reader?
4. How much time did you spend last week reading the Sony Reader?
5. What did you like about reading text on the Sony Reader?
6. What did you dislike about reading text on the Sony Reader?
7. How would you change or improve the Sony Reader?

These questions were asked with the objective of understanding how the first-year students would use the Readers, whether their use would encourage reading as a more focused activity, whether reading would become a mobile activity for the students, and how the students themselves thought the devices fit (or did not fit) into the academic environment and their lives. In addition to participating in the surveys, the students were required to publish a weekly blog post on a topic relevant to the class's discussion of that week (post topics were assigned by the instructors). Although the students were not specifically asked to blog about their Sony Readers, some of what they said in their blog posts was revealing about both the devices and the students' views of reading and books.

Evaluation of student surveys and blog posts revealed that, above all, reading is an intensely personal experience, and thus opinions about the Sony Reader's features were varied and often in conflict with one another. Despite this, the data collected did reveal some themes that remained fairly consistent from student to student. One hypothesis at the beginning of the study was that students might refrain from multitasking while reading on the Sony Reader because it is a unifunction device. However, only 37% of the students in the first year seminar class did not engage in other activities while reading (Figure 2). Although the Sony Reader is a mobile device, most of the students used it only in their dorm rooms (Figure 3). Although they were not asked why they chose a particular location, this choice may have been due to the proximity to other necessary materials, such as notebooks and computers. Across the board, students' time spent reading on the devices was fairly minimal. Analysis of the surveys individually shows that several students did not use the readers at all, and that reading time declined as the semester progressed. Finally, although none of the students used this word in describing what would make the device better, their responses indicated that there is a desire for greater *interaction* with the text (e.g., abilities to highlight passages), as well as multi-media support for other functions from the device. Overall, the students were glad to have tried a Sony Reader but indicated that the devices would need to show significant improvement in functionality before they would be feasible in an academic setting.

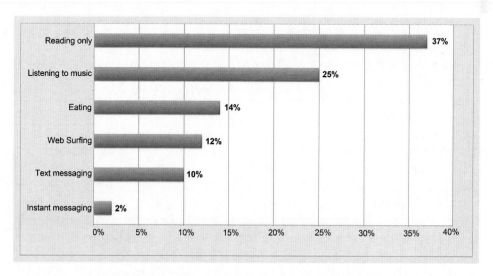

FIGURE 2 Student activities while using the sony reader.

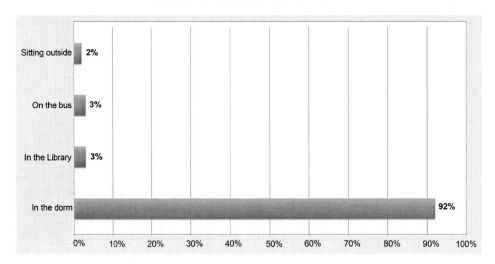

FIGURE 3 Where students read the sony reader.

English Preliminary Findings

This phase of the study considered two primary issues—how the digital reader engages a student in immersive reading practices and how the loss of the paper-bound book influenced students' reading habits. The second question specifically asked the students to evaluate the digital reader.

The 48 student participants in the English 30 classes were asked a series of approved interview questions over five interview sessions. The interviews were taped and remain a part of the research archives. The following questions were asked of each participant.

1. What have you liked the best so far about using the Sony Reader in this class? What have you liked least?
2. How has the Sony Reader changed, or not, when and where you read the texts assigned for this class?
3. How has the Sony Reader changed, or not, how you read the texts assigned for this class?
4. Do you tend to remember the texts you read in the Sony Reader better or worse than texts you read in codex form? Is there a difference?
5. Have you loaded texts not assigned for this class onto your reader?
6. Has your reader helped you do the research necessary to write the papers for this class?
7. In what ways has reading on the Sony Reader been the same or different than reading a codex book? Do you miss any of the features of a codex book?
8. What types of texts seem to be best suited to the Sony Reader? Which seem to be least suited?

9. Are there any features that you wished the Sony Reader had to make your reading more productive or enjoyable?
10. Is reading on your Sony Reader different than reading on your computer? In what ways?
11. Are there any texts that you wish you could load onto your reader, but can't? Why can't you load them?
12. Have you printed out any of the texts that you have loaded onto your Sony Reader? Why have you printed them?
13. Have you used your Sony Reader in concert with other digital devices? Which ones and how?
14. What changes would you suggest to make the Sony Reader more efficient?

The students' semester-end presentations reflected the findings of the recorded interview sessions. The respondents believed that e-readers are here to stay and that learning to navigate digital content on these new reading devices is becoming an essential skill. In general, the students felt that the digital reader would enhance their reading experiences by creating access to reading materials that otherwise may not be available or limited through traditional print text. Most saw the advantages of using readers as a central access point for all of their reading materials, eliminating the need to carry multiple books and saving on the cost of copying. The "eco-friendliness" of the Readers appealed to everyone.

Many students viewed the Reader as yet another device in the cache of reading tools—somewhere between a print text and a computer. Generally, students indicated that they read at night, but at times they were unable to complete the assignment because their Reader had lost its charge. A majority of respondents requested a backlight be installed on a future generation of the reader.

When using a digital reader, students found they read differently. They described the experience as more like reading a printed text than reading on a computer screen but felt the reader had a long way to go to make it feel like a "real book."

Are E-readers Ready for Us?

Although the title of this article is "Are You Ready For E-readers?," the results of the Penn State Sony Project indicate that a better question might be "Are E-readers ready for us?" It was evident throughout the Sony project that e-readers are not yet the perfect reading device for the academic environment. Although the functionality of highlighting, notetaking, and bookmarking is improving, the technology is far from where it needs to be for these devices to replace of the traditional book. Will e-readers ever replace paper books? Students consistently reported that they do not have the same "relationship" with or feeling for their e-readers that they have with a codex book. This may change as e-reader technology improves and becomes more widely adopted.

There seems to be a new e-reader on the market every day, from the Kindle to the Nook to the new iPad. The question increasingly becomes not how to make any particular technology or device work in an academic library, but how to offer content that will work for every device our patrons might choose to use.

The Penn State University Libraries' Sony Reader project has provided a much better understanding of the ways that our students and faculty want to use electronic reading devices and why they may choose to do so. The project team strives to maintain a finger on the pulse of our patrons' ever-changing content, format, and device needs. In addition, the team has developed a set of best practices that would serve any institution well in testing new devices with their user populations. These include:

- Learn about copyright and terms of use policies for devices and make sure to be in compliance with these policies or contact the company to seek exception for the purposes of your project.
- Work through your institution's institutional review board for any studies you wish to do, insuring compliance with university policies.
- Provide training or help sheets and FAQ resources for users.
- Be aware of accessibility accommodations—work with your institutional review board and with your university office for disabilities to insure compliance and appropriate accommodation for students who need it.

As both purchasers and providers of content, libraries have the opportunity to play a major role in the future of e-content and the devices on which that content is accessed. Librarians have the power to form partnerships and initiate conversations between our institutions and publishers, vendors, and device creators to advocate for our users in enabling access to content in multiple formats on multiple devices. Perhaps the involvement and influence of libraries in the e-book and e-reader realm can help create a positive future where the paths of the devices and the content will meet up to provide the ultimate e-reading experience.

REFERENCES

Abel, David. 2009. "A Library without the Books." *The Boston Globe*, September 4. http://www.boston.com/news/local/massachusetts/articles/2009/09/04/a_library_without_the_books/.

Antolini, Tina. 2009. "Digital School Library Leaves Book Stacks Behind." *NPR,* November 9. http://www.npr.org/templates/story/story.php?storyId=120097 876.

Behler, Anne. 2009. "E-readers in Action: An Academic Library Teams with Sony to Assess the Technology." *American Libraries* 40: 56–9.

Clark, Dennis T. 2009. "Lending Kindle E-book Readers: First Results from the Texas A&M University Project." *Collection Building* 28: 146–9.

Demski, Jennifer. 2010. "The Device versus the Book." *Campus Technology* 23: 27–33.

Kho, Nancy Davis. 2010. "E-readers and Publishing's Bottom Line: The Opportunities and Challenges Presented by the Explosion of the E-reader Market." *EContent* 33: 30–5.

Kiriakova, Maria, Karen S. Okamoto, Mark Zubarev, and Gretchen Gross. 2010. "Aiming at a Moving Target: Pilot Testing Ebook Readers in an Urban Academic Library." *Computers in Libraries* 30: 20–4.

No Shelf Required. http://www.libraries.wright.edu/noshelfrequired.

Rodzvilla, John. 2009. "The Portable E-book: Issues with E-book Reading Devices in the Library." *Serials* 22: S6–S10.

Left to Their Own Devices: The Future of Reference Services on Personal, Portable Information, Communication, and Entertainment Devices

THOMAS A. PETERS

TAP Information Services, Oak Grove, MO

The mobile revolution, the fastest diffusion of technology in human history, is rapidly changing the future of reference services. Using personal, portable information, communication, and entertainment (PP ICE) devices to ask and receive reference information is not just another in the growing list of reference communication channels. PP ICE reference fuels mobile information experiences, which are integrated more closely with what one is doing and thinking at the moment. To be useful in the mobile era, library reference services need to overcome the reference desk mentality and the schedule fetish. Because of the mobile revolution, social search will rise again.

INTRODUCTION

Reference services delivered as text chat (short message service [SMS], a form of text messaging on mobile phones) and media (multimedia messaging service [MMS]) to portable devices differ in some fundamental ways from reference services delivered at a desk, over the phone, through the Internet, or even in virtual worlds, such as Second Life. The questions often are more sensitive, contextual, and "directional" in ways not often seen in the other reference channels. The mobile revolution, the fastest diffusion of any technology (that is, anything created by humans) in history, is redefining the future of library reference services in some fundamental ways. To deliver quality mobile reference services to mobile users, libraries, other organizations, and collaborative efforts involving individuals need to offer 24/7 services with rapid turnaround time (less than 10 minutes on average), a relaxed yet authoritative style, and an attitude that treats all questions with respect, including questions involving requests for opinions and advice.

The impact of the mobile phone revolution alone dwarfs all other computer and network advances, from the first personal computer to the Internet to the iPad. Over the past 10 to 15 years, mobile phones have experienced a rapid and extensive adoption and diffusion around the globe. The International Telecommunication Union (ITU), a United Nations agency based in Geneva, Switzerland, estimates that the number of mobile phone subscriptions will reach 5 billion in 2010 (http://www.itu.int/net/pressoffice/press_releases/2010/06.aspx). ITU estimates that there were 4.6 billion mobile cellular phone subscriptions worldwide at the end of 2009—67 for each 100 citizens, if those subscriptions were evenly distributed (http://www.itu.int/ITU-D/ict/publications/idi/2010/Material/MIS_2010_Summary_E.pdf). Approximately 60 of the countries of the world (approximately 31%) already have achieved 100% mobile phone saturation. In other words, there are as many cell phone subscriptions as people in those countries.

The diffusion of mobile phones is arguably the fastest diffusion of any technological device in human history, and the breadth of the diffusion is surpassed by only a few constructed things, such as clothing, shelter, eating utensils, and television sets. Mobile phones are quickly becoming as popular in developing countries as in developed countries. ITU estimates that at the end of 2009 there were 57 mobile cellular subscriptions for every 100 inhabitants of developing nations, increased from 23% penetration as recently as 2005 (http://www.itu.int/ITU-D/ict/publications/idi/2010/Material/MIS_2010_Summary_E.pdf).

Although mobile phones may be used most heavily by tweens (a preteen who is between childhood and the fully teenage years) and teens, all age ranges and socioeconomic classes now use mobile phones. We truly are in the midst of a global mobile revolution.

However, to fully appreciate the extent and implications of mobile reference services, we need to consider all types of personal, portable information, communication, and entertainment (PP ICE) appliances, including netbook and tablet computers, dedicated eReading devices, portable music and media players, portable gaming devices, and all of the portable devices designed for children. Libraries need to strive to make their services accessible to all mobile users, regardless of the device, operating system, and service plan. The days of dominance by one model or device type (e.g., the black rotary phone or the Model T Ford) probably never will visit the realm of PP ICE devices.

To make sense of the effects of the current mobile revolution on information services, we need to consider what can be mobile in this context, as well as our sense of place. Humans, of course, are mobile creatures. We move around with notable regularity using a wide variety of conveyances. During the typical reference desk encounter, the patron must "lug the guts" (Harbage 1969, 959) to the reference service point from across town, across campus, or from within the library. Human mobility can be measured in person-miles.

The total number of person-miles undertaken per year probably increased dramatically in the last half of the 20th century, due in part to a general increase in the standard of living and the maturation of transportation systems supporting automobile and air travel. Long, extended trips became relatively commonplace in a way that would have astounded, say, a Victorian.

In the 21st century, because of the current mobile revolution, the number of person-miles may actually plateau or decrease, not so much because of increasing travel costs but because we can now accomplish so much on our mobile devices without having to lug the guts to some service point. As humans, we will continue to move around to our favorite homes and haunts, but the mobile revolution may paradoxically result in a decline in the total number of person-miles traveled each year. We will not cease to move around, but our movements may become more deliberate and less far-flung.

This could have a profound effect on our collective sense of place, especially one's local environs. The history of such a vague thing as our collective sense of local place is difficult to define and determine, but the industrial revolution and the subsequent transportation revolution almost certainly redefined our collective sense of local place. In the United States, as getaway weekends and snowbirds hauling their RVs to Florida, Texas, and Arizona to avoid the cold Northern winters became popular, the sense of being tethered to some local environ became attenuated. The mobile revolution may enable most of us to continue to understand ourselves as citizens of global communities of interest while at the same time reviving a pre-industrial sense of (and appreciation for) our particular local place. With the full diffusion and adoption of the PP ICE revolution and a concomitant return to a pre-industrial sense of place, computerized information networks, which first created the liberating sense of a library without walls and eventually seemed to threaten foot traffic in libraries (lugging the guts, again), may result in a revived interest in and use of local libraries and other familiar, close homes and haunts.

Documents (text-bearing devices) can be mobile, too. This is the basic fact that interlibrary loan, Amazon's pre-Kindle business model, and NetFlix's pre-streaming delivery service have in common. They and many other services were all about taking the documents to the people rather than making the people come to the documents. We can call the mobility of documents "lugging the pulp" (because paper, not plastic or vellum, remains the defining medium of this general historical period) to distinguish it from "lugging the guts" to the location of the documents of interest.

However, mobile documents do not really change how people use the documents once they have been delivered. A printed book received via interlibrary loan is used in much the same way as a book plucked from the shelf of a nearby library. The mobility of documents is a wonderful thing, but this mobility does not intrinsically alter how humans interact with individual documents or individual kernels of information. Through the mobility of documents, there are just more kernels available to any individual information seeker, and more chaff to winnow.

Communication can be mobile, too, of course. This began when people started hollering across valleys, and it quickly escalated to include semaphores used by ships at sea, transatlantic cables, the Internet, and more. Informal mobile communication seems to be what has fueled the enormous and rapid diffusion of mobile phone subscriptions around the globe. People thought of communicating with family, friends, and colleagues long before they considered using their mobile phones to ask reference questions to a library, order a pizza from the local pizzeria, or any other form of formal individual-to-organization communication.

PP ICE devices are more than just another in the long line of library communication channels. They seem to have unleashed a wide variety of mobile information experiences, many of which are new ways of creating, interacting with, and using information. Many types of mobile information experiences are very dynamic and interactive. Consider the library user in Oklahoma who, during a recent night of severe weather, lost electrical power to his home. No lights and no computer, but he still had his cell phone with a charged battery and the My Info Quest (My IQ) SMS-based library reference service's number (66746) either memorized or saved on his phone. Calling his local library on a landline would not have been useful (assuming the reference desk at the local library was still open) because the electrical outage was widespread. Therefore, this library user sent a query asking when the local electric company estimated that power would be restored to his area.

The My IQ collaborative SMS text-based mobile reference service has been operational for more than a year. Over 50 libraries and library-related organizations and several "rogue" librarians such as myself (i.e., librarians not directly employed by any single library) have been "staffing the desk," monitoring the short questions (usually fewer than 160 characters) that are typed in as text chat by users of mobile phones from wherever they are and whatever their information need of the moment is. One user had locked himself or herself out of his or her house and used the service to locate the closest locksmith. Many users use My IQ to ask directional questions as they are on the move. Because the only thing the My IQ service provider knows for sure is the cell phone number of the user and the 160 characters or less sent as an SMS-based text message, any assumptions made about the demographics of the My IQ user population are just inferences. However, based on the general topics and modes of expressing questions, many users appear to be teenagers.

After serving as a My IQ service provider for a year and thinking about my experiences in light of my prior reference service experiences providing service at reference desks, over the phone, on the Internet, and even in the three-dimensional virtual world called Second Life, I have developed a personal (perhaps idiosyncratic) list of key points about the fundamental affordances of SMS-based mobile reference services that libraries and librarians need to understand and embrace to realize the full potential of the mobile reference revolution—in other words, to serve the mobile population (two-thirds of the world's population and growing) truly well. Although these ideas, trends, and affordances are numbered for convenience, they are in no particular order of importance.

SOCIAL SEARCH SHALL RISE AGAIN

There are at least three basic sources of information: other people, the environment, and documents (perhaps four, if we include supernatural sources of information—God, gods, spirits, E.T.). For a long stretch of human history, environmental search (e.g., sticking your head out of your cave to determine the current weather) and social search (e.g., asking your spouse to stick his or her head out of your cave to determine the current weather) were the dominant ways of gathering information. Then documents came along and libraries developed, resulting in "library search" as a third way of finding information. Reference service as traditionally conceived and implemented was primarily a form of human-mediated library search. The librarian helped the user find information in documents (or at least catalogs, indexes, and documents likely to contain the information sought). Sometimes a reference encounter will tap into the social search network of a campus, organization, or community but document search seemed to dominate. In all of my years of providing reference service, I cannot recall a single instance where I used environmental search to answer a patron's information need.

Then computerized information networks, the Internet, and the World Wide Web came along and search engines were born. Search engines such as Google and Bing are primarily about searching through documents and files to find needed information. The power and efficiency of online catalogs, electronic databases, and search engines really tipped the scales heavily in favor of library search as the primary way of finding information. In comparison, social search "engines" were fairly rudimentary. Some people used e-mail and e-mail discussion groups as a type of social search engine, posing questions and information needs to the entire group, hoping that someone or a few people would respond with useful information. Environmental search engines, such as traffic, seismic, and weather monitors and networks, advanced as well but not nearly at the same pace and with the same impact as library (document) search engines.

The mobile revolution may result in the re-ascendancy of social search as the dominant type of information search. Some may say that social search has a rightful place at the top of the information search heap, and that the rise to dominance of library (document) search in the modern industrial era and the first decades of the computerized network era was just an aberration—fluke of the disproportionate technological develops that allowed library search to eclipse social search and environmental search. Aardvark and other new mobile reference services may be game-changers in the sense that they primarily look to other people, not to documents, as sources of information. Aardvark, now owned by Google, appears to have created a social search algorithm that makes it easy, fast, and efficient to find another person or just a few (not all of the subscribers to an e-mail discussion list) who can quickly meet your information need. Speaking at a TEDxSoMa event in San Francisco on January 22, 2010, Damon Horowitz from Aardvark noted, "The primary goal of [information] technology should not be to replace human intelligence, but rather facilitating human interaction" (http://www.youtube.com/watch?v=1YdE-D_lSgI). Despite the fact that library reference services were at least partially into social search before a social search became cool again, there are some fundamental problems with library reference services, as traditionally conceived and delivered. Unless we rethink and redesign library reference services to better meet the information needs of the mobile legions, library reference services will become marginalized and much less valuable to the population served.

OFFER THE SERVICE 24/7

The mobile digital era demands 24/7 service from most sectors of our culture, society, and economy, including banking, healthcare, and information services. The restaurant sector is one where the 24/7 moniker raises suspicions and doubts, not reassurance. Unless your library is very large (e.g., the Library of Congress or the New York Public Library) or unless your reference service providers are insomniacs, offering a 24/7 SMS-based text reference service cries out for collaboration, preferably with some libraries, library-related organizations, or rogue librarians with local homes and haunts on other continents.

RESPOND IN LESS THAN 10 MINUTES

If your reference policy and procedure manual contains some statement such as "We will respond to your submitted question within one business day," run, don't walk, to the master copy of the manual and change that to 10 minutes. Users of a SMS-based text reference service are using their cell phones to ask questions. Their questions occur in the context of other text-message conversations with which they are currently engaged. If you do not respond in a matter of minutes, not hours, the context will be lost and the need will be diminished or satisfied in other ways. Also, in your response include an inkling of the question as a gentle reminder to the mobile patron. For example, if a patron texts, "How old is Oprah?" do not respond merely with the correct answer (56) but rather in a way that implies the question: "Oprah is 56 yrs old."

LOSE THE REFERENCE DESK (AND THE REFERENCE DESK MENTALITY)

The reference desk service mentality is great (or at least good) for physical reference desks in bricks and mortar libraries, but it can be limiting when thinking about mobile reference services. For example, approachability is an entirely different can of worms when a reference service is delivered over a mobile phone or other PP ICE device. You need to think about the advantages and costs of using short codes rather than full ten-digit phone numbers and the type, memorability, and uniqueness of any keywords you ask patrons to input with their text-messaged questions. Another aspect of the reference desk mentality that needs to be rethought is the assumption that at any given moment only one or a few members of the reference team is "on the desk" providing service. Mobile technology is a two-way street. The librarians can be as mobile as the users. One evening I used my mobile phone to answer incoming My IQ questions while I watched my son play baseball. Having high-speed Internet access on a larger device clearly is better and easier at present than trying to answer SMS-based text questions on a smartphone, but that playing field may soon become level or even tilted in favor of the truly PP ICE device.

LOSE THE SCHEDULE (AND THE SCHEDULE FETISH)

Developing and maintaining a "desk" schedule is the biggest time drain of a mobile reference service. Planning and scheduling, we lay waste our powers (with apologies to William Wordsworth). Future mobile reference services will use something akin to Aardvark's social search engine to locate a member of the designated reference team who seems to be awake, responsive, and capable of answering a specific question. It will be liberating. Thinking back to the 1980s, I still recall with fear and loathing the questions about business and government documents that I, the humanities reference librarian, was required to field because the schedule dictated that I was "on the desk." In the smart mobile reference era, questions will be routed to the service provider best equipped to answer them. End of schedule.

OVERCOME THE GREAT CHAIN OF REFERENCE QUESTIONING

The Great Chain of Being "is the idea of the organic constitution of the universe as a series of links or gradations ordered in a hierarchy of creatures, from the lowest and most insignificant to the highest. . ." (Wiener 1973, 325). A 1579 drawing of the Great Chain of Being by Didacus Valdes (http://www.stanford.edu/class/engl174b/chain.html) shows God at the top of the chain and Satan at the bottom, with angels, humans, other creatures, plants, and rocks marshaled along the vertical continuum. In a similar vein, reference service as traditionally conceived (at least in academic libraries) often seems to imply a Great Chain of Reference Questioning, with in-depth reference needs as the top followed by ready reference questions, citation verifications, and directional questions. Questions involving requests for advice or opinions often are relegated to the infernal, subterranean regions.

For library-based, SMS-based text reference services delivered to smartphones and other PP ICE devices to survive and thrive, we need to overcome or abandon the Great Chain of Reference Questioning. Based on one year of service in one collaborative service of this type, it seems that many questions are indeed directional or are asking for advice or opinions. This may be partly due to the nature of the communication medium (remember, most people make the great leap to a mobile phone to communicate with friends and family, not to ask reference questions) and partly due to the implicit demographics of the user population (primarily teens and young adults).

PROVIDE OPINIONS AND ADVICE IN A PROFESSIONAL, DISINTERESTED MANNER

Users are expressing the need for opinions and advice delivered via mobile reference services. As a profession, we need to discuss how to respond to that need. For example, we can politely choose to ignore or redirect those types of questions. (Go seek advice and opinions elsewhere.) On the other hand, we could use emerging mobile social networks to try to help mobile users locate advice and opinions. Of the making of five-star rating systems, there is no end. For example, we could respond to a "safe" question about which of the 20 novels Author X has written is the best by noting that her third novel has the highest aggregate reader rating across umpteen online five-star rating systems. If someone wants to know if Poppy's Pizzeria in Paducah, Kentucky, is worth a visit, we could perhaps refer the person to the current FourSquare Mayor of Poppy's because he or she has proven to be a frequent customer.

TREAT ALL TEXT-BASED QUESTIONS WITH RESPECT

However, what if the question involving a request for advice takes this form (as it did for me), "What is the best way to have anal sex with my girlfriend?" Such a question quickly replaces all thoughts of good books and pizza. Quite a few questions that are sent to the My IQ service could be interpreted at least initially as frivolous, pranks, or beyond the scope of the service. The My IQ service providers have agreed to assume that all incoming questions are asked in earnest and to treat them with respect. There are in fact several guides to anal sex available on the World Wide Web that can be summarized in 160 characters or less. Perhaps I'm just old and clueless, but I have a hard time imagining many people using a walk-up reference desk or a telephone (voice) reference service to ask these types of intimate questions. SMS-based text reference service creates the distance and anonymity whereby these types of questions can be asked and answered.

This article is based on some early experiences and wild-eyed imagining about what mobile reference could become and mean. Even in these early halcyon days, there may be trouble in paradise. For example, if social search overtakes library search as the dominant way to seek information, how can we be sure that a group of MLS-brandishing librarians will provide a better mobile reference service than some other group of individuals, even individuals who self-select to serve as service providers from a crowd-based mobile reference service (such as Aardvark)? How can we establish and maintain a professional deportment and distance in a mobile social search service? Do we even want to do that? How is that serving the users of the service? We need to have a fresh conversation in librarianship about the meaning and value of professionalism in the era of ubiquitous mobile computing.

Although reference services delivered to and by smartphones will not entirely replace other established modes of reference service (desk, voice, chat, World Wide Web, or virtual world), mobile reference is not just one more addition to the growing list of reference service technologies. It is forcing all of us (providers and users of such services) to rethink and reimagine mobility, information seeking, and our sense of place. In the mobile era, users are being left to their own devices. And that's a good thing.

REFERENCES

Wiener, Philip P., ed. 1973. *Dictionary of the History of Ideas: Studies of Selected Pivotal Ideas*. New York: Charles Scribner.

Harbage, Alfred, ed. 1969. *William Shakespeare: The Complete Works*. New York: Penguin.

Mobile Technology and Medical Libraries: Worlds Collide

PEG BURNETTE

Library of the Health Sciences-Peoria, University of Illinois College of Medicine, Peoria, IL

Use of mobile technology in medicine has steadily gained momentum over the past 10 years. With the advent of new mobile devices that offer superior functionality and connectivity, medical librarians have an opportunity to expand mobile services and resources that have the potential to enhance user experience, medical education, and clinical practice. This article looks at the genesis of mobile medicine from the early adopters to today's always connected user.

INTRODUCTION

If you are a medical practitioner, educator, or librarian, medical informatics is on your mind or it should be. As an important component of informatics, mobile computing represents the information gathering paradigm for the next decade. To plan for future mobile resources and services, it may be helpful to understand how medicine and handheld technology got together. It was in the mid-1990s when the medical library and the personal digital assistant (PDA) first met. Their story is relatively short but significant as the medical community embraced the potential of these small devices and ultimately changed the very nature of medical practice, medical education, and medical librarianship. The relationship that began quietly and simply quickly grew and evolved into an intense and enduring partnership.

The adoption and market penetration of mobile technology was serendipitous and somewhat unexpected. In the case of handhelds, what began as a device of convenience for the business community has become an indispensable tool for medical students, residents, nurses, practitioners, and even patients. With rapid and continuous improvements in mobile technology, medical institutions and libraries are challenged to adapt and respond accordingly.

LOOKING BACK

It is no surprise that the early versions of personal organizers failed to gain a foothold. Released in 1993, the Apple Newton, with its clunky physique and short battery life, fell short of expectations and was never widely adopted. However, physicians took notice. In 1994, Dr. Steven Labkoff of Harvard Medical School used Apple Newtons for his Constellation Project. This project looked at residents' attitudes toward the devices and their use for clinical practice.[1] As part of the project, software engineers developed a search tool for the Newton that would retrieve articles related to drug information. Sandeep Shah, lead developer for the project, continued on his own to further develop the search platform, ultimately founding Skyscape, a major vendor of mobile software for medicine.[2]

Several developers involved in the Newton project left Apple to continue development of the handwriting recognition software. They expanded the project to include hardware, and in 1996 the Palm Pilot was released. In 1998, following the sale of Palm to 3Com, the founders of Palm left to found Handspring, the first of several companies to license the Palm operating system. Like the early Palm Pilots, Handspring Visors were monochromatic, powered by AAA batteries, and had 2 to 4 MB of memory. Microsoft entered the handheld market on the heels of Palm with the Windows CE operating system. Compaq used this platform for the first iPaq.[3,4]

These small handheld devices, which became known as Personal Digital Assistants (PDAs), were initially marketed to busy professionals as personal information managers. The device connected to the user's computer via cradle or cable using serial or USB connections. Software on the computer facilitated the transfer of data and applications through a process called synchronization. The user could also add data to the device using a stylus to tap on-screen buttons or icons or an on-screen keyboard. The stylus could also be used to fashion letters directly on the screen. Later models boasted built-in Bluetooth, WiFi connectivity, or both and some featured a qwerty keyboard. Expansion options included modems, cameras, external keyboards, and voice recorders. A program called Margi-Presenter-to-Go facilitated PowerPoint presentations from a handheld that could connect directly to a projector.

MAJOR PLAYERS EMERGE

Even as multiple developers entered the handheld market, Palm and Microsoft emerged as early industry leaders and competitors. New and improved versions of their respective operating systems were released regularly. There were several widely acknowledged differences between the two operating system devices. Palm devices (which included the Palm, Handspring, and Sony models) were generally smaller and lighter with superior battery life. They were easy to use and were generally less expensive. The Windows Pocket PC operating system replaced Windows CE in 2001. Windows CE/Pocket PC devices, which included the iPaq and Dell Axim, were bigger and heavier, but they also had larger color screens and, for windows users, the interface was familiar. Battery life was not as good and they tended to be more expensive. There were significantly more medical applications for the Palm OS, many of them freeware, which no doubt contributed to the popularity of Palm devices among physicians, residents, and medical students.

ALONG CAME A SMARTPHONE

Smartphones, also called feature phones or multimedia phones, were somewhat slower to take hold. Early models were either glorified cell phones with calendar and calculator functions or they were PDAs with less than satisfactory phone functionality. They were more expensive than a PDA, and the user had additional monthly phone charges and Internet access fees. Symbian and Linux operating systems offered additional options, but it wasn't until 1999 when Research in Motion (RIM) introduced the first BlackBerry that competition heated up. BlackBerrys became affectionately known as "Crackberrys" because users became addicted to their superior connectivity and e-mail interface.

However, with the introduction of the iPhone in 2007 Apple permanently changed the mobile computing landscape. Google's more recent Android platform and the resulting Droid phones are sure to be major players in what feels like a new mobile computing market.

WHY MEDICINE?

As a physician, resident, or medical student in the early 1990s, your lab coat would typically be weighted down with a Merck manual, a Washington manual, and one or two other pocket guides, a few laminated cheat sheets, and a pregnancy wheel, not to mention your cell phone and pager. A very non-scientific experiment suggested that the weight of these items could easily approach five pounds.

Physicians started to think about ways handhelds could be used to access information for clinical practice as soon as the devices appeared. Early programs were mostly homegrown, stand-alone applications such as MedCalc, MedMath, and ABG Pro. These were developed for Palm devices and were freely shared. For several years, Palm applications far outnumbered those for Windows CE/Pocket PC.

ePocrates, a free drug resource developed specifically for the handheld, was released in 1998 and quickly gained wide-spread popularity. ePocrates was marketed on the premise that it was updated weekly, delivering the latest drug updates, warnings, and alerts with each synchronization. ePocrates developers have continued to enhance and expand the product, including versions for newly released operating systems. It remains one of the most used medical handheld applications.

Publishers and software developers created handheld-friendly versions of major medical texts, such as the 5 Minute Clinical Consult and Harrison's Principles of Internal Medicine. As hardware evolved, web-based point of care products, such as MDConsult and InfoRetreiver, were offered in mobile formats. The dynamic nature of these applications and their frequently updated content drove the shift in PDA device use from a stand-alone reference tool to a more interactive, connected one.

The diffusion of the medical handheld was at first fueled by medical students and residents who tended to be younger and more comfortable with technology. After all, the PDA was not very different from a Game Boy. Physicians, particularly older ones, tended to be more wary of technology in general. However, anecdotally, preceptors and attending physicians were impressed by the immediate results when a student or resident used one of these portable reference gadgets. Those who were not intimidated eagerly joined the PDA user community. Medical schools encouraged, and some even required, their students to purchase PDAs. Some programs used PDAs to track student activity such as patient encounters. Many residency programs provided monetary support for interns to purchase a handheld. Adoption in the field of nursing has been a little slower; however, handheld technology is now an important part of nursing education and practice.

ENTER THE LIBRARY

Physicians were not the only ones to see the potential of handheld technology. Medical librarians saw a role for libraries as well, including the provision of hardware or software, instruction, PDA Web pages, technical support, user groups, seminars, and product fairs. The decision to support mobile technology was a serious commitment with serious obstacles but also rewards.

For libraries that chose to loan hardware the challenges were many. Criteria for device selection included operating system, connectivity, synchronization, security, screen size, weight, expansion, cost, and availability of software. One could choose to limit support to only one operating system, but even within the same operating system new devices were being developed so quickly that by the time a library purchased and processed hardware it was already yesterday's technology.

The logistical questions were many. Were the devices cataloged? Would a device be loaned with or without the synchronization tools that included a cradle or cable to connect the device to a computer? Would the library install software on the device or allow users to install software of their own choosing? If a user let the device run out of power all content was lost and had to reinstalled. Would users be allowed to load personal address books or calendar information? How were the devices wiped of personal information before being loaned to the next user? Users unfamiliar with the technology, and in the early years that was most, would need instruction. Would the library provide synchronization stations? Doing so usually required working closely with the institutional IT department, adding yet another layer of complexity.

The Library of the Health Sciences-Peoria (LHS-Peoria) became actively involved in medical PDAs in 2001. During the first pilot project, we loaned a Handspring Visor, including all the accessories, to each third-year student (M3) for their six week Internal Medicine rotation. Each student also received a copy of Harrison's Manual of Medicine and the Washington Manual on expansion cards designed specifically for the Visor. Due to the popularity of this trial (students were reluctant to return the devices at the end of the six weeks), the College of Medicine elected to purchase a Visor for each M3 the following year. The library was tapped to manage the whole project, which included pre-loading the devices with ePocrates, MedCalc, and MedMath and providing all training and support. The devices were collected at the end of the year and were redistributed to the M3 class the following year.

Another lending model was to loan devices, with or without software, for short periods of time to users who wanted to test drive a device before purchase. LHS-Peoria employed this model in a 2002 project in which we partnered with OSF Saint Francis Medical Center Library and Resource Center. During the "Point of Care to your Palm" grant, we purchased Handspring Visors and Pocket PCs that were then preloaded with subject-specific software also purchased for the grant. We also offered peripherals such as keyboards, cameras, voice recorders, and Margi Presenter-To-Go. The commitment to provide and support handheld services and resources was not taken lightly. This project was a huge undertaking in largely uncharted territory. Library staff became the recognized PDA experts on campus, elevating the library's visibility particularly with off-campus faculty and residents. The project also served as an opportunity for faculty collaboration, allowing us to form lasting relationships that led to new roles for librarians in the curriculum.

Equally challenging was how to provide the software. At the very least, it is essential that librarians have access to devices to evaluate the software. Beyond standard evaluation criteria, such as authority, quality, accuracy, scope, timeliness, and audience, it was also necessary to consider format, interface, navigation, ease of use, procurement, licensing, and cost.

Colleen Cuddy discusses five models for providing medical software and licensing issues related to each. Options include stand-alone free or fee-based titles, licensed stand-alone titles, products bundled with existing institutional licenses, products with a finite number of downloads, and publisher or vendor discounts.[5] After product selection, method of delivery, licensing, updates, technical support, cataloging, and use tracking require careful consideration. Libraries involve themselves in the medical PDA movement in other ways as well. Web pages point users to information about hardware and software and might include recommendations or subject-specific lists of titles. Some libraries provided stations where users could regularly synchronize PDAs. PDA user groups, symposia, technology fairs, and general technical support elevated the role of the library while connecting to users in ways not seen before.

LOOKING FORWARD

This brings us to today's lab coat. The coat hasn't changed much, but what is in the pockets certainly has. Today's resident typically uses an iPhone or Droid phone with ePocrates and other select medical reference resources installed. This phone provides Internet access for e-mail and browsing and also acts as a pager.

We are leaving behind the era of the PDA and moving into Mobile Computing and Mobile Medicine. Ironically, early handheld devices were always "mobile" but not necessarily "connected." Today's mobile label implies mobility with connectivity. In addition to anytime, anywhere learning, mobile devices have conjoined personal and professional lives into one little device that for many is a virtual lifeline. Personalization persists as each user has unique and specific expectations and needs.

Today's devices have better screens, faster processors, longer battery lives, and 24/7 connectivity. Because they are connected, it is easier to download content directly or use web-based resources wirelessly. A few holdouts remain who prefer the two-device model, one handheld as a reference resource and a separate cell phone. However, most users are finding the smartphone the best of both worlds.

So, how do libraries continue to engage users in the mobile environment? Today's user is always mobile and connected and expects access to anything at any time from anywhere. However, that information tends to be temporary as users want access only as long as the information is useful and then it is replaced with something else.

Opportunities remain for libraries to provide content and services to the mobile user. Typical mobile services include catalog search, request or renewal of materials, and SMS reference. A mobile-friendly Web site will soon be a given. Digital collections that can be searched and accessed remotely allow the user to take advantage of the bulk of library collections from any location. Consider what your users want and what will give you the best return on investment. Investing in product development that provides access to content that the majority of your users don't care about may not be worthwhile. On the other hand, doing so could serve as a model of development, access, and delivery. Lessons learned will translate into better functionality the next time around.

For clinical practice, medical libraries can leverage themselves as content experts by pointing practitioners to the best information and resources for evidence-based patient care. Instruction and technical support should be a part of this endeavor. SMS is an opportunity to connect with users in ways beyond basic reference. Assign students and residents to a personal librarian who is available to answer questions for virtual rounds. Use SMS to push information such as alerts or updates for research interests.

Developing mobile applications from scratch is problematic because of the variance in operating systems and devices. Libraries generally don't have librarians to write programs for a specific platform such as iPhone or Android. However, libraries can take advantage of existing tools. Weekly or monthly podcasts can alert users to new resources or important medical updates. Instructional videos, or virtual library tours, can be made available on iTunes or YouTube in formats that are user-friendly and easily accessible. Rurik Greenall discusses in-depth the benefits of Web-based content as a more realistic and attainable service approach.[6]

Providing access to library-licensed tools allows users to take full advantage of point-of-care (POC) resources that can be used on the Web or on a mobile device. These POC tools not only provide valuable information for the practitioner but many also include excellent patient care materials.

Keeping up with the mobile technology is enormously challenging. Here are a few web sites that provide up to date information on development.

- Mobile Libraries: http://mobile-libraries.blogspot.com/2009/07/mobile-technologies-in-libraries.html
- M-Libraries: http://www.libsuccess.org/index.php?title=M-Libraries
- Engadget Mobile: http://www.engadgetmobile.com/

- Epocrates Go Mobile "Bedtime Reading": http://www.epocrates.com/gomobile/bedtime-reading.html
- Palm Doc Chronicles: http://palmdoc.net/

CONCLUSION

Is mobile medicine still relevant for libraries? Much of the research points to the benefit to the practitioner. Although research also suggests a potential benefit for patients when physicians use PDAs, that information has been more elusive. Common sense would dictate that the physician who is equipped with relevant information at the point of care (POC) makes better clinical decisions and by default that improves overall patient care. Concerns have been raised about the rapid increase of handheld technology in medicine, citing lack of proof of benefit and fear of potential harm.[7] However, that could be argued both ways. Are we not obliged to employ technology that anecdotally has substantial benefit? Would it not be unethical to ignore this technology because there is not yet substantive "proof"? If the question is about the efficacy and reliability of POC resources, then that is a bigger issue and one not limited to mobile computing. Like any process, the information retrieved and ultimately used is in large part a function of the competency of the end user. Let's not blame technology for the misuse of the information that it provides. So it falls to librarians to do what we have always done: provide our users not only with information but also with the tools they need to find and evaluate information in support of education, research, clinical practice, and life-long learning.

NOTES

1. Stephen E. Labkoff, Sandeep Shah, Joseph Bormel, YoonJoon Lee, and Robert A. Greenes, "The Constellation Project: Experience and Evaluation of Personal Digital Assistant in the Clinical Environment." *In Proceedings of the Annual Symposium on Computer Application in Medical Care* 1995: 678–82.

2. "Fifteenth Anniversary of Leadership in Mobile Medical Information," Skyscape Team, accessed May 28, 2010, http://www.skyscape.com/Company/Anniversary.aspx (no longer accessible)

3. Jeff Dodd, "A Brief History of PDAs," PDAs 9, no. 7 (2003), http://www.smartcomputing.com/editorial/article.asp?article=articles/archive/10907/21107/21107.asp&guid.

4. Thomas A. Peters, Jo Dorsch, Lori Bell, and Peg Burnette, "PDAs and Health Sciences Libraries," *Library Hi Tech* 21, no. 4 (2003): 400–11.

5. C. Cuddy and P. Wrynn, "Licensing Content for PDAs," *Journal of Electronic Resources in Medical Libraries* 4 (2007): 175–84.

6. R. T. Greenall, "Mobiles in Libraries," *Online* 34 (2010): 16=–9.

7. Kenneth De Ville, " 'The Cure Is in Hand?' The Brave New World of Handheld Computers in Medicine," *Cambridge Quarterly of Healthcare Ethics* 17 (2008): 385–400.

Methods for Applied Mobile Digital Library Research: A Framework for Extensible Wayfinding Systems

JIM HAHN

Undergraduate Library, University of Illinois at Urbana-Champaign, Urbana, IL

MICHAEL TWIDALE and ALEJANDRO GUTIERREZ

Graduate School of Library and Information Science, University of Illinois at Urbana-Champaign, Champaign, IL

REZA FARIVAR

Department of Electrical and Computer Engineering, University of Illinois at Urbana-Champaign, Urbana, IL

Navigation within the physical library building can be supported with mobile computing technology; specifically, a path suggestion software application on a patron's mobile device can direct her to the location of the physical item on the shelf. This is accomplished by leveraging existing WiFi access points within a library building as well as supplementing wireless infrastructures with additional wireless beacons for collections-based wayfinding.

INTRODUCTION

The purpose of this article is to communicate the results of collaborative planning among researchers from the University Library, the Department of Computer Science, and the Graduate School of Library and Information

Science at the University of Illinois Urbana–Champaign. The plans articulated here are for applied research with handheld technology, leveraging the library's wireless infrastructures to produce a novel software application. The mobile software application enables library patrons to navigate the print collection as they search for items identified from the online catalog. The proposed wayfinding software will enable library patrons to use their mobile devices to locate multiple service points within the library complex as well as libraries across campus. The project is based on WiFi fingerprinting, a technology for determining the position of a device in a building even when GPS-based localization is unavailable.

This article will communicate methods and a framework for research in collections-based wayfinding with handheld technology; this is essentially a blueprint to the future researchers in digital libraries for building an extensible framework for wayfinding systems in libraries and cultural institutions of all types. By "extensible," we mean that components of the software system can be used as needed, and we do not advocate a one-size fits-all approach for any cultural institution. The wayfinding needs of a large academic research library with multiple service points and collection locations will differ from those in a small one-room, rural library. The research here specifies methods for advancing library wayfinding for multiple library types and does not leave any cultural institution behind in a future of massive ubiquitous access to information with handheld technology.

The planning for this research used as its hypothetical test site the campus libraries of the University of Illinois, located in central eastern Illinois. There are more than 30 departmental libraries in the University of Illinois Library system with more than 12 million volumes, making it the largest publicly funded research university library in the United States in terms of collections.

LITERATURE REVIEW: PREVIOUS LIBRARY WAYFINDING RESEARCH

The planned research is an extension of previous work on collections based wayfinding applications at the University of Oulu in Finland, where wayfinding work is operational. This research at Oulu allowed mobile device users to perform a catalog search from their phone, and then be guided to the location of the book in that library with a positioning engine leveraging wireless infrastructure of the library (Aittola, Ryänen, and Ojala 2003; Aittola, et al. 2004). In their articles, the engineering researchers in Finland cite the work at the Cornell HCI lab, which built prototype mobile computing systems in which test users could take tablet-sized computers into the stacks and use the online catalog to search from their location in the stacks. They include in their prototype "a mapping device that directed you to the book in the stacks" (Jones et al. 2000, 98). Similarly, a group at Virginia Polytechnic Institute and State University completed prototype work for library navigation using WiFi and mobile devices in a research project on location-aware systems in libraries (Sciacchitano et al. 2006).

The First International m-libraries conference in 2007, followed by a 2009 international conference, provided renewed impetus for the library and information science field to take notice of the emerging mobile learning trend within education and distance learning. These conferences have been invigorating to the m-library research community with practice-oriented reports and solutions for librarians supporting users at a distance. The conference presentations show how the Library and Information Science (LIS) community has been involved with provisioning library resources for mobile devices, which are in important ways distinct from traditional desktop computing (International M-Libraries Conference 2008). Although prototype initiatives discussed earlier do exist, these projects have not moved beyond the stage of early adopter libraries and experimental services. At this time, mobile navigation for in-library engagement is not yet a robust service offering for libraries and mobile services provisioned based on location have not yet gained widespread adoption.

A presentation by the mobile research group at North Carolina State University claims that the next directions for mobile device service development include "Discovery of digital library content across collections using current location as a filter" (Nutter, Sierra, and Wust 2008, slide 22). The WolfWalk mobile initiative (http://www.lib.ncsu.edu/dli/projects/wolfwalk/) provides new ways of engaging with digital content by providing access to the digital images of the library's collection based on user location on campus. The interesting aspects of mobile technology are made possible by the fact that the devices are portable and suited for engagement with the surrounding environment. This all underscores the importance of the proposed software project at Illinois. The MobiLib group sees any location outside of the library as context for recommending digital resources. We believe that mobile digital resources should not preclude the possibility of invigorating the on-site library experience.

USER NEEDS

Consider the knowledge and skills of the first-year undergraduate student as she begins her studies at the university. With a conceptual framework for understanding public libraries and high school collections, this student is unaware of the breadth of the vast collections of a research library available digitally and in print. This platform can deliver a compelling library navigation tool for students new to university study. National surveys in the perceptions of libraries (de Rosa 2006) indicate that "Borrowing print books is the library service used most" (de Rosa 2005, 6-3), and that the "Library Brand" is books (de Rosa 2006, 3-1). The path suggestion software proposed here would deliver to students increased access to their most valued library resource.

The *College Students' Perception of Libraries and Information* report indicates that most college library users "have not asked for help using any library resources, either at the physical library or the virtual library" (de Rosa 2006, 6-4). Because almost every undergraduate student carries a cell phone, a handheld wayfinding system is suited to give undergraduate students the independence they desire while navigating information resources in the library. Library users in large library settings run the risk of falling victim to the "last mile" syndrome—they know something exists in the Library but they do not have sufficient information or bibliographic skills to physically locate precisely what they need from the collections and services offered.

TECHNOLOGY

The main goal of this project is the development of an application that provides real-time directions to a physical resource specified by the user. The application, running on a mobile device, should be able to locate the current position of the user within a library building and direct her to the desired resource. To achieve this goal, we will create a stable and user-centered service platform for library wayfinding in the Undergraduate Library space. Our plans are to produce a library positioning service operational on one device—the Apple iPhone. This objective specifically addresses the overall research question: How best to design, deliver, and assess a wayfinding application for mobile devices?

Our system will provide an inexpensive way to automatically maintain the most reliable and stable fundamental information required by in-door localization systems, including the map of the signal strength in an area and location of books within the physical collection. To increase accuracy of wayfinding, we plan a multi-tiered infrastructure solution (depending on building variability) of WiFi fingerprinting in an autonomous mobile system that collects WiFi signal strength surveys and additional signal beacons, such as the integration of RFID tags and RFID readers in the physical library.

WiFi Fingerprinting

WiFi fingerprinting works in two phases. The first phase (training) records the signal strength received at different locations. The set of signal strengths and the location at which the sample has been taken are stored in a database. Once a large enough set of signal strengths is collected, users can locate themselves by observing the strength of the access point signals received in their current location and comparing it with the ones recorded in training: the location of the user can be determined by looking at the location with the most similar set of signal strengths.

There is a rich body of research on this topic (Farivar et al. 2009; Krishnan et al. 2004; Ladd et al. 2002) guaranteeing the feasibility of this underlying technology. Moreover, this technology has been researched and a basic prototype is implemented showing the practicality of the WiFi fingerprinting technology. There is research work underway on methods of improving the accuracy of WiFi fingerprinting, both in the client phone's software through advanced statistical modeling and as additional access points placed strategically in a building to improve the wireless signal behavior in the spots of the building where location finding accuracy is below average.

To implement WiFi fingerprinting techniques, the first step is to build a wireless signal map of the target building, in this case the Undergraduate Library. This map will show the signal and noise strength of separate WiFi access points at each location of the building. Once the map is created, the next step involves application of preprocessing algorithms to prune unwanted or ill-behaving access points. Once the data is preprocessed and formatted, the data will be incorporated into client devices, thus finishing the data-training phase. During application deployment, a client device can observe the set of signals it can sense at a certain location in the building and using the collected signal behavior data across the building can deduce its location with certain accuracy.

The majority of WiFi fingerprinting literature focuses on the online phase of estimating a user's location using a previously created fingerprint map. From our own experience in deploying a wireless localization system in several buildings in a six-month span (Farivar et al. 2009), generating and updating the wireless map is a nontrivial problem and should not be overlooked. WiFi signal strength in an office environment changes over time because new access points are introduced in or removed from the environment and furniture gets moved around. In many buildings, the wireless channel propagation characteristics are continually changing (due to continually changing environments and infrastructure), and WiFi fingerprint maps are quickly rendered stale, leading to inaccurate location estimates mere weeks after the map creation. This problem is multiplied if there are a large number of predetermined locations.

In Bahl, Padmanabhan, and Balachandran (2000), the authors propose a solution of creating multiple maps, reflecting different possible channel conditions. Access points compare the received signal strengths of transmissions from each other to choose the best map to use in the online phase. This is updated as channel conditions vary. However, a chosen map may not accurately approximate the channel conditions at a given time because the environments change drastically and in an unpredictable manner. In Krishnan et al. (2004), the authors introduce additional transmitters and receivers in the physical space at well-known fixed locations. The transmitters periodically broadcast packets. The receivers listen for these packets, as well as mobile users' packets, to refine the fingerprint map when estimating the location of users. Like Krishnan et al. (2004), our solution will introduce additional wireless infrastructure.

Radio Frequency Identification (RFID)

RFID is the use of an object (typically referred to as an RFID tag) applied to or incorporated into a product, animal, or person for the purpose of identification and tracking using radio waves. RFID technology is used in many localization technologies. For example, Hahnel et al. (2004) use a mobile robot to determine the locations of fixed tags in space. This creates an RFID map that the robot uses to localize itself, as well as to track the movements of other mobile objects. Similarly, in Bohn and Mattern (2004) the authors embed tags in the floor, similar to our set up. A small mobile vehicle equipped with an RFID reader moves through the field of tags randomly. As it scans the tags, it creates a map of the field. Other mobile vehicles can use this map to navigate through the tag field. In Loffer et al. (2008), the authors store the location information in tags. They also store metadata, such as the building and neighborhood. This information is displayed on tag interrogation on a mobile device.

Mobile Computing Technology

Mobile devices offer the ability to further extend the navigation for users by offering integrated data capture affordances, such as barcode reading through the phone's camera, RFID, and smart card readers. For several years, our research group has been developing applications for both the iPhone and the iPod touch (devices running the iPhone OS) and for devices running the Android operating system.

Overall System

The environment we are targeting is an open library collection, the book stacks of the Undergraduate Library. Users typically navigate the collection by the use of call number shelf arrangement. Should students choose to use this mobile wayfinding system, they will be presented with two options:

a. They will have the option of downloading and running our wayfinding software if they have a mobile device that satisfies the infrastructure requirements.

b. If that is not the case, they will be able to borrow a library mobile device containing our software.

The overall system will be composed of readily available commercial components. To meet the RFID infrastructure needs, a Touchatag™ RFID reader (http://www.touchatag.com/home) with the respective RFID tags will be used. The mobile device will be connected to data from an RFID reader in charge of reading a set of RFID tags embedded in known fixed positions. These fixed positions include the room's access points, bookshelves, and book collections. The overall operation proceeds by directing to the specific room, followed by section of the room, followed by bookshelf in that section. As a final step, the user will be directed to a particular section of the bookshelf by following the embedded RFID tags in each of the books. It is at this point where the users would finally achieve their goal of obtaining a desired item from the collection. Alternatively, the patrons will be presented with the proper metadata redirecting them to additional sources of information, which may be digital (online research databases and digital collections) or print material (books that exist in the physical building), related to the topic of immediate interest. The system will have the capability to respond to users' individual needs within the context of the collection.

ASSESSMENT OF WAYFINDING SOFTWARE WITH RAPID PROTOTYPING

There are several challenges in developing a successful, useful, usable, and indeed used wayfinding system. We can build on the experiences of prior systems, including those noted above. We can also draw on the literature describing traditional non-computational wayfinding activities in physical libraries—how patrons navigate within and between floors and shelves to get to the books they want (Eaton 1991). The problems of physical layout and signage are a valuable starting point in understanding the needs that people have (Eaton and Taylor 1992). The questions asked of librarians, library staff, and fellow users are indicative of the types of problems that people have in navigation, the typical breakdowns that occur, and the supplemental needs that people have. This creates the initial requirements for the first prototype. However, with such a novel technology it is unwise to assume that this is a straightforward process of determining requirements, designing, implementing, and deploying a system, and then conducting a study to demonstrate that the system is a success. The traditional software engineering waterfall model will fail in such a context because there are far too many unknowns.

We have already noted the challenge of understanding people's requirements for functionality for such a device, and the intended process for beginning that requirements capture process. But that is indeed just the beginning. Novel technologies are complex and confusing and raise addition challenges in developing both the functionality and the interface:

- What is it that people actually want from such a device?
- How much can we reliably learn by asking people what they want?
- What if they may want something, but it never occurs to them to ask for it because it has never been available or affordable before?
- How much can we gain by understanding how people cope with existing navigation challenges?
- Of the many features we might build into the application, what is the subset we should build for our first version?
- Which set of features will have the biggest impact given a limited budget?
- Which set of features will serve as a useful proof of concept and allow us to learn more in order to build a better version?
- How easy will it be for people to learn how to use the application?
- How easy will it be for people to use the application?
- How do people cope when things (inevitably) go wrong with the application?
- Can people understand failures caused by poor network connections, software errors, or the book simply not being in the right place – or do they blame themselves?
- How useful will people find the application?
- Will they keep using it after the novelty wears off?
- Will they recommend it to their friends?
- Once they have the application, will people discover new uses for it that they and we have not thought of?
- Once they have the application, will people want yet more features that they cannot imagine until they have actually used the first version?

These challenges can seem daunting. However, they are common in the development of any new technology that has the potential to change and improve what people do. We believe that the best way to address such challenges is by rapid iterative analysis, design, and evaluation. That is, to develop an early prototype and ask people to test it out for us on authentic tasks (the types of things that they typically do, rather than tasks we have invented) to show off the amazing power of our system regardless of how improbable it is that a real person would ever want to do that task.

This is not a simple matter of sending people off with the application, asking them to do something and then fill out a questionnaire saying how wonderful they thought our application was. Rather it requires involving the users in an ongoing conversation about what was easy, what was hard, what was confusing, what was surprising, and what they wished they could have done with the application to directly address their underlying information needs – even as those needs kept on evolving in the light of interacting with the application, the library and the information resources it contains. Such an evaluation is inherently qualitative and formative. It necessarily focuses on problems (what went wrong and what needs fixing) rather than on the successes of what seems to work. It requires in-depth interaction with users and consequently is only feasible with small numbers of participants.

This type of situated evaluation inevitably uncovers new design challenges that must be addressed in the next version, followed by further evaluation and analysis. Such a process requires that each stage of the iteration can be completed sufficiently quickly that it is easy and affordable enough to "fail fast," learning from our mistakes and uncovering the hidden subtleties of the larger design problem as we go.

Various techniques of rapid prototyping already exist to help this process. However, we will also need equally rapid analysis and evaluation techniques so that iterations can cycle through as soon as possible. That means that more rigorous experimental and definitive evaluation protocols are too slow and expensive. Instead, we advocate for several small scale but in-depth studies, involving just a few people and focusing on discovering the most important issue that needs to be fixed in the next iteration.

Over multiple iterations, this approach allows for the building of a robust understanding of the way that features, interfaces, the particular setting, and the varying needs and prior expertise of participants have an effect on what people do and their experience of interacting with the application.

CONCLUSION

The importance of this research is underscored by its ability to make use of the unique attributes of mobile technology: portability, ubiquity, and wireless capabilities. It is because the devices themselves are carried by the library patrons as ubiquitously as they would carry their wallet or purse that these devices can be leveraged to create an invigorating on-site library experience. The design for mobile use in library settings is advanced by using the attributes of mobile computing that make them distinct from desktop computing.

REFERENCES

Aittola, M., Tapio Ryänen, and Timo Ojala. 2003. "SmartLibrary – Location-Aware Mobile Library Service." Proceedings of the Fifth International Symposium on Human Computer Interaction with Mobile Devices and Services, Udine, Italy, September 8–11. Accessed May 14, 2010. www.rotuaari.net/downloads/publication-2.pdf.

Aittola, M., Pekka Parhi, Maria Vieruaho, and Timo Ojala. 2004. "Comparison of Mobile and Fixed Use of SmartLibrary." Proceedings of the 6th International Conference on Human Computer Interaction with Mobile Devices and Services, Glasgow, Scotland, September 13–16. Accessed May 14, 2010. www.rotuaari. net/downloads/publication-28.pdf.

Bahl, Paramvir, Venkata N. Padmanabhan, and Anand Balachandran. 2000. "Enhancements to the RADAR User Location and Tracking System." Microsoft Research Technical Report. Accessed May 31, 2010. http://research.microsoft. com/pubs/69861/tr-2000-12.pdf.

Bohn, Jürgen, and Friedemann Mattern. 2004. "Super-Distributed RFID Tag Infrastructures." In *Proceedings, Ambient Intelligence Second European Symposium, EUSAI 2004, Eindhoven, The Netherlands, November 8–11*, edited by Panos Markopoulos, Berry Eggen Emile Aarts, and James L. Crowley, 1–12.

de Rosa, Cathy. 2005. *Perceptions of Libraries and Information Resources: A Report to the OCLC Membership*. Dublin, OH: OCLC Online Computer Library Center.

de Rosa, Cathy. 2006. *College Students' Perceptions of Libraries and Information Resources: A Report to the OCLC Membership*. Dublin, OH: OCLC Online Computer Library Center.

Eaton, G. 1991. "Wayfinding in the Library: Book Searches and Route Uncertainty." *RQ* 30: 519–27.

Eaton, G., and M. Taylor. 1992. "Evaluating Signs in a University Library." *Collection Management* 16: 81–102.

Farivar, R., D. Wiczer, A. Gutierrez, and R. H. Campbell. 2009. "A Statistical Study on the Impact of Wireless Signals' Behavior on Location Estimation Accuracy in 802.11 Fingerprinting Systems." Paper presented at IEEE International Symposium on Parallel & Distributed Processing, Rome, Italy, May 23–29.

Hahnel, D., W. Burgard, D. Fox, K. Fishkin, M. Philipose. 2004. "Mapping and Localization with RFID Technology." Paper presented at the IEEE International Conference on Robotics and Automation, New Orleans, Louisiana, April 26–May 1.

International M-Libraries Conference, Mohamed Ally, and Gill Needham. 2008. *M-libraries: Libraries on the Move to Provide Virtual Access*. London: Facet.

Jones, M. L. W., Robert H. Rieger, Paul Treadwell, and Geri K. Gay. 2000. "Live from the Stacks: User Feedback on Mobile Computers and Wireless Tools for Library Patrons." Proceedings from the 5th ACM Conference on Digital Libraries, San Antonio, Texas, June 2–7.

Krishnan, P., A. S. Krishnakumar, W.-H. Ju, C. Mallows, and S. N. Gamt. 2004. "A System for LEASE: Location Estimation Assisted by Stationary Emitters for Indoor RF Wireless Networks." Paper presented at INFOCOM 2004, Twenty-third Annual Joint Conference of the IEEE Computer and Communications Societies, Hong Kong, March 7–11.

Ladd, Andrew M., Kostas E. Bekris, Algis Rudys, Guillaume Marceau, Lydia E. Kavraki, and Dan S. Wallach. 2002. "Robotics-Based Location Sensing Using Wireless Ethernet." In *Proceedings of the 8th annual International Conference on Mobile Computing and Networking*, 227–238. Atlanta, Georgia: ACM.

Loffer, A., U. Wissendheit, H. Gerhauser, and D. Kuznetsova, 2008. "GIDS: A System for Combining RFID-Based Site Information and Web-Based Data for Virtually

Displaying the Location on Handheld Devices." In *2008 IEEE International Conference on RFID*, Las Vegas, Nevada, April 16–17.

Nutter, S., Tito Sierra, and Markus Wust. 2008. "Libraries and the Mobile Web." Digital Library Federation Fall Forum 2008, Board of Trustees Meeting, Providence, Rhode Island, November 12, 2008. Accessed May 14, 2010. http://www.lib.ncsu.edu/dli/projects/mobilib/dlf-fall-2008-board.ppt.

Sciacchitano, B., Chris Cerwinski, Ivan Brown, Miten Sampat, Jason Chong Lee, and D. Scott McCrickard. 2006. "Intelligent Library Navigation Using Location-Aware Systems: The Newman Project." In *Proceedings of the 44th Annual Southeast Regional Conference*, 371–376. Melbourne, Florida, March 10–12.

One Block at a Time: Building a Mobile Site Step by Step

CHAD HAEFELE

Davis Library, University of North Carolina at Chapel Hill, Chapel Hill, NC

In August 2009, the University of North Carolina at Chapel Hill Libraries launched a mobile web site and catalog designed for use on smartphones. Library users can search for books and view library hours, location branches, and other basic information about the University of North Carolina libraries on their iPhone, Android phone, or other smartphone. An outline of the development process is given in eight major steps that are designed to be replicated by other libraries. Lessons learned during development are also shared, along with recommendations of devices to develop for and tools to use.

INTRODUCTION

In August 2009, the University of North Carolina at Chapel Hill (UNC) Libraries launched our mobile website, designed for smartphone use (UNC Libraries 2009). Although mobile web development can seem intimidating, it in fact relies on some basic decisions and skills that are transferable from more traditional web site design. Although our development process was different in some ways from building a traditional desktop browser web site, the resulting challenges were easy to overcome.

The iPhone's release in 2007 heralded a new age of mobile web use. By loading webpages quickly and displaying them just as on a desktop, the iPhone's Safari browser was more usable than many alternatives. Previous web-enabled phones often repackaged the web for viewing on smaller screens, with varying results.

Since 2007, other smartphones have answered the iPhone's challenge by updating their browsers. Android, some Palm, and some BlackBerry devices all have very usable web browsers. An increasing subset of the general population of library users now own those smartphones, and that number is predicted to pass 50% in late 2011 (Nielsenwire 2010). However, although desktop-style webpages are usable on smartphones, they sometimes fall short of an ideal experience.

A 3.5-inch screen is large compared to some other devices but still tiny when placed next to any desktop or laptop monitor. Text on a smartphone screen is usually readable, but that reading experience leaves much to be desired. In addition, not all smartphone browsers have equivalent capabilities. A webpage that displays perfectly on one device may be a blank page or string of error messages in another.

At UNC Chapel Hill, we anecdotally noticed an increase in smartphone ownership rates among our students and faculty dating from the iPhone's release. In mid-2008, users began to occasionally make a webpage loaded on their smartphone part of their reference question. Looking at those loaded pages, it quickly became obvious that our web site's current design did not always meet the needs of mobile users. Usability issues were confirmed by experimentation with staff-owned devices. Our web site, while functional, was not easy to use on a smartphone.

A mobile web site project was quickly launched, and the initial development effort took from March 2009 to the site's launch in August 2009. We learned much about mobile web development, including which considerations are important to take into account when designing a mobile web site. Based on our development process, these lessons can be broken down into a series of eight building blocks.

BLOCK #1: SURVEY YOUR USERS

Although we had anecdotal evidence of users accessing our site with mobile devices, we needed structured data to guide our efforts. Was smartphone use an actual extrapolated trend among our users or did we just happen to encounter the few diehards? In addition, we knew that smartphone compatibility issues existed and wanted to make sure any development effort targeted devices used by the majority of our users.

In March 2009, a simple multiple choice poll appeared on the main page of UNC's Davis Library. It asked one question: "Which mobile device do you use most?" Available answers were "iPhone/iPod Touch," "Android Phone," "Blackberry," "Treo," "Nokia N95/N96," and "Other," with a text field to elaborate on what "Other" is.

TABLE 1 Which Mobile Device Do You Use Most?

Device	Responses	Percentage
iPhone / iPod Touch	102	48.6%
Android Phone	2	.9%
Blackberry	57	27.1%
Treo	3	1.4%
Nokia N95/N96	2	.9%
Other	44	21%
Total Responses	210	

Source: Online survey conducted on http://www.lib.unc.edu/davis/, March 2009.

Of 210 responses, 48.6% answered "iPhone/iPod Touch," 27.1% responded "BlackBerry," and results dropped sharply from there. See Table 1 for full results.

One other response statistic is notable: 21% selected "Other." Although a small minority of these 44 responses were obvious jokes, like "Carrier Pigeon," many others indicated use of "plain" or "cheap free" simpler phones. Of our users who use mobile devices, slightly more than one-fifth did not have a smartphone. This served as a reminder during our development process, pointing out that whenever possible we should make sure our mobile site was usable on both new and older devices.

Note in particular that this survey was conducted in the spring of 2009. The mobile landscape has changed significantly since then and will continue to do so. Given the increase of Android ownership into the second place position (NPD Group 2010), I would expect Android usage rates to be substantially higher among our users if we ran the same poll again today. However, although this data may no longer be entirely accurate, the point stands that it is absolutely necessary to get some type of picture of your users' mobile web browsing habits before developing a mobile site.

BLOCK #2: PLATFORM

After learning what devices our users owned and used, the next step was picking a platform to develop for either the iPhone, Android, Palm, or something else. And on top of that, should we develop an app or a webapp? Based on the survey data, we decided to focus primarily on iPhone compatibility and make it additionally compatible with BlackBerries whenever possible. Although this decision was data-driven, the app or webapp choice was made more out of necessity.

An app is roughly analogous to a traditional desktop computer application. It is written in a programming language, such as Objective C or Java, then compiled and installed on the smartphone. A webapp is simply a webpage optimized for display on mobile devices. It can be written in virtually any standard web coding language (e.g., HTML, javascript, or PHP).

Apps and webapps each have advantages and disadvantages. Generally speaking, apps can access more of a device's hardware than a webapp. If a camera is required to accomplish a task, this can usually only be accomplished in an app. However, an app also requires substantial investment in expert programmer time. In addition, an app can only be used on the device it was programmed for. An iPhone app can not be used on an Android device, or vice versa. To target a comprehensive user base, app coders must maintain multiple versions of their app in different programming languages.

Writing a webapp is comparatively much simpler; anyone with even basic web development experience can produce a mobile webapp that will work across multiple smartphone platforms. However, that webapp will not be able to make use of the phone's camera or other hardware capabilities.

In some ways, an app or webapp can be the simplest choice to make in the mobile development process. It comes down to a basic question of what resources are free to work on a project. If no expert programmer time is available, then an app is out of reach, but as mentioned previously, even a beginning web developer can produce a mobile webapp. A fully installed app was beyond the capabilities of programming resources we had available, so by default we focused our development on a webapp.

Still, not all mobile browsers are created equal. A webpage created with one device in mind might not function completely as desired on another. The next stage of platform choice was picking which browsers to develop for. Thankfully, many smartphone browsers are similar enough to each other that coding with one in mind produces a site usable on others. The iPhone and Android browsers in particular are very similar. At UNC, our choice to focus on the iPhone meant that our resulting site also worked on Android devices. Covering just these two device types provides access to a percentage of smartphone users that, while broad, can at first seem deceptively small. Table 2 shows market share and mobile web traffic share of various mobile devices. In February 2010, RIM (the manufacturer of BlackBerry devices) held 42.1% of U.S. smartphone subscribers (comScore 2010). So why not focus on BlackBerries if they alone make up so many potential users?

TABLE 2 Market Share and Web Traffic Share of Smartphones

	Market share (smartphone subscribers), Feb. 2010	Mobile web traffic share, March. 2010
RIM (Blackberry)	42.1%	7%
iPhone	25.4%	39%
Google (Android)	9.0%	46%

Sources: comScore 2010; AdMob Metrics 2010.

Although more BlackBerries have been sold, iPhone and Android users have substantially higher rates of mobile web use in the United States. Despite being owned by so many customers, BlackBerries comprise just 7% of mobile web use, whereas the iPhone accounts for 39% and Android another 46% (AdMob Metrics 2010). Based on similar statistics available during our development process, focus on BlackBerries was downgraded and the iPhone became our primary development platform. As a first effort, it is a better strategy to target users likely to actually browse a mobile web site than to provide an unused capability to a broader population of BlackBerry owners.

A webapp allows use across multiple devices, whereas an app does not. With limited resources available to the project, a webapp was our logical choice to reach the highest possible percentage of users. Our following choices ensured that our webapp would function correctly on iPhones, Androids, and assorted other devices.

BLOCK #3: FRAMEWORK

A framework is a collection of tools designed to simplify the development process. In the case of mobile web development, a framework often consists of CSS, javascript, and image files. Together, these files handle much of the overhead in designing for a smaller mobile screen. A framework handles the interface, freeing developers to focus on producing content in mobile-friendly forms. Assuming that a webapp was chosen over an app, the next decision to make was selecting a framework.

It is certainly possible to develop a mobile website freehand, without a framework's assistance. This approach would in fact provide greater design flexibility. However, our limited resources in programmer time were again a prime consideration, and use of a framework substantially lowered the barrier to entry in mobile web development.

One example framework was developed by Jason Clark, the head of Web Services at Williams College Libraries. His code, a product of his own research into mobile web development, is available for free on his web site (Clark 2009). Figure 1 is an example of what this framework looks like in use.

Another framework is iUI, an open source project hosted on Google Code (Google Code n.d.). iUI was developed to "Provide a more 'iPhone-like' experience in your Web apps" (Google Code n.d.). In fact, iUI displays correctly on devices beyond the iPhone. At UNC, we chose to build our site with iUI. It displays correctly on iPhones, Android phones, the Palm Pre, and some BlackBerries. Figure 2 shows our mobile site as an example of an iUI interface. iUI's Google Code introduction page is helpful in getting the

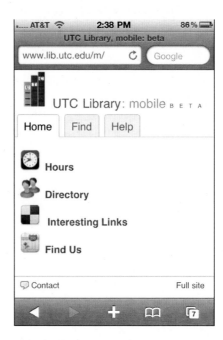

FIGURE 1 The University of Tennessee at Chattanooga's mobile Library website. http://www. lib.utc.edu/m

FIGURE 2 UNC Chapel Hill's mobile Library website. http://www.lib.unc.edu/m

framework up and running, and the project has a very active user community to help with any issues encountered.

Other frameworks exist as well, these are just examples. The best way to choose a framework is to sit down and experiment with a few. See what they look like on various devices, and think about how their user experiences relate to what your organization wants to accomplish with a mobile site. I highly recommend trying a framework on an actual mobile device or a desktop emulator instead of loading it in a desktop web browser. Mobile frameworks are sometimes highly focused on smartphone browsers and may not display correctly in a desktop environment.

BLOCK #4: DATA SOURCES AND OUTSIDE SYSTEMS

It's easy to forget that creating a mobile web site also creates additional maintenance tasks. If both the mobile and non-mobile versions of the library's web site have a Library Hours page, then staff suddenly has an extra place to update and maintain that information. An extensive mobile site will create an equally substantial increase of web site maintenance tasks.

For this reason, mobile site updates should be automatic whenever possible. If library hours information is pulled from a database, then the process can be streamlined. Both the mobile and non-mobile library hours pages can pull data from the same database, a source that has to be updated just once. When deciding on content for a mobile site, make a list of what information your organization has stored in databases or other such sources that can be used to automate content updates.

North Carolina State University built a system that displays computer availability information to students on their (non-mobile) webpage; because this information is pulled from a database, they were able to easily reformat it for mobile screens (North Carolina State University n. d.). At UNC, we maintain a database of our electronic resources. We also have a list of electronic resources with mobile-friendly interfaces on our mobile site. The mobile site's list is not currently pulled from the database and requires manual updating. As more vendors add mobile capabilities, maintaining the list has become a difficult task. We are in the process of switching over to a database-generated list that will save substantial time.

Other non-database sources can also be automatically pulled into a mobile site without manual updating. RSS feeds are an excellent example. Our News & Events blog's RSS feed is automatically translated into a mobile-friendly format. Our Libraryh3lp IM reference system also provides a mobile-friendly interface, which we easily integrated into the mobile site. All of this content updates automatically, without need for staff time. Not all content can be syndicated in this style but making use of the feature whenever possible will save staff time and headaches in the long run.

BLOCK #5: CUSTOM CODE

Now that the structure of a mobile site is in place, make a list of what content you would like to include in the mobile site that isn't possible to automate. Those pieces are the custom code necessary to write. Using the iUI framework, our custom code for the basic site was fairly minimal. Almost all of it was done in simple HTML.

Our philosophy when choosing what content to write in custom code was to pick information that answers very quick questions. Although further study is necessary to confirm our assumption, at this point we do not believe that users want to do in-depth research on a smartphone. They might want to find out library hours and branch locations but will not sit down and begin building a bibliography on their phone. Along those lines, we selected our site sections, seen in Figure 2.

BLOCK #6: CATALOG

At this point, the focus of developing a mobile site was been largely on static, non-interactive content. Our site was originally designed to answer simple questions, such as whether the library was open or how to contact us. However, as we began to beta test the site and gather user feedback, one question came up over and over again: How do I search the catalog? Both students and faculty mentioned a use case of searching for a call number on a smartphone while lost in the stacks. Aligning with our previous assumptions in producing mobile content, they wanted a quick book lookup, not in-depth Boolean searching.

A mobile catalog is a feature that quickly showed users the utility of a mobile site, and one they were asking for. Although not essential to a mobile site, if possible a mobile catalog interface should be included. There are three major options for establishing a functional mobile catalog:

1. Purchase a vendor-supplied interface. This is the simplest option because the library's existing ILS vendor does all the work. An example is III's Airpac interface (Innovative Interfaces n.d.). A list of vendors who provide mobile interfaces is available on the LibSuccess wiki (Farkas n.d.).
2. Purchase a third-party product. In this case, the library would pay a vendor to add mobile capabilities to the catalog. This method is just as easy as option one, and a great choice when your ILS vendor does not have a mobile interface available. LibraryThing's Library Anywhere product is an excellent example (Spalding 2010).
3. Build a mobile catalog interface yourself. Building from scratch is the least expensive option but also the most time-intensive. Building your

own mobile catalog assumes that you have access to your catalog's raw data in some form (XML or otherwise).

At UNC, we were fortunate and had access to our catalog data as XML feeds. The exact method of how our catalog was built is beyond the scope of this article, but lacking a direct XML feed an option is to explore PHPYAZ. PHPYAZ is a product that can pull data into a usable format from any Z39.50 compliant source (Index Data 2008).

Building a custom mobile catalog takes time and programming, but for us the results were worth it. An interactive catalog answers basic information needs in ways that static information cannot. Our users often praise the mobile catalog's usefulness, and our marketing and promotion of the mobile site now frequently refers to the entire site as the Mobile Catalog.

BLOCK #7: PROMOTION

Like any new library service, a mobile web site needs promotion for users to know it exists. The standard array of posters, bookmarks, and newsletter blurbs still apply, but mobile sites have a unique way to let the most likely potential users know that the site exists—by displaying a notice to mobile users when they visit the non-mobile site. We do this on all UNC Libraries webpages. A few lines of CSS code make sure that our notice ("On a mobile device? Visit http://www.lib.unc.edu/m") only appears on mobile users' screens. The CSS is very simple code and is widely supported (Wisniewski 2010, 56).

Going a step further, it is also possible to skip displaying that message and automatically redirect mobile users to the mobile site. The choice of methods is up to each individual organization, but implementing either one will greatly increase your mobile site's visibility to those already using smartphones to browse the library's site.

BLOCK #8: EVALUATE AND ITERATE

No mobile web site is ever complete, just as no non-mobile website is ever finished. A mobile site can be pushed out in a very bare bones state without negative reaction. Even a simple list of hours is helpful to mobile users and will likely be much more readable than the non-mobile version of the page.

But any mobile site, no matter how simple or complex, should contain a link back to the non-mobile version of the site. Because mobile sites tend to be a subset of information available on the larger non-mobile site, few will serve every conceivable information need from a mobile user. Providing a link back from a mobile to non-mobile interface will keep users from getting frustrated or feeling trapped in the mobile site.

Once a framework and basic content are up and running, begin adding other pieces of content. Look at statistics and see what is most popular on the site when choosing where to focus future development.

We learned one surprising fact in particular from our mobile site's stats: the majority of traffic to the mobile site comes from non-mobile browsers. The reason for this is currently unknown. Do users prefer the simpler mobile catalog interface over our regular one and choose to use it on their desktop computer? Or are they just trying the mobile site out of curiosity? Questions such as this may be part of a future usability study.

Any mobile site is preferable to none, even if it is not perfect. Users will appreciate the more convenient browsing and understand that more is coming later. We have added several features since launch, including a text message export option from the mobile catalog, an expanded list of smartphone-friendly library resources, and the ability to search the catalog via barcode scan.

CONCLUSION

Smartphone ownership rates are increasing. As our users become more familiar with browsing the web on smartphones and other mobile devices, libraries need to be ready to meet their needs in this new space. Although establishing a mobile presence can seem a daunting task, breaking it down into smaller tasks and individual decisions can help direct developers. Using development of the UNC Libraries' mobile web site as an example, there are eight major blocks in development:

1. Survey your users
2. Platform
3. Framework
4. Data sources and outside systems
5. Custom code
6. Catalog
7. Promotion
8. Evaluate and Iterate

REFERENCES

AdMob Metrics. 2010. "March 2010 Mobile Metrics Report." Accessed May 25, 2010. http://metrics.admob.com/2010/04/march-2010-mobile-metrics-report/.

Clark, Jason. 2009. "Mobile Web Design—Working Code, Tips, Best Practices." *DigInit*, November 13. http://diginit.wordpress.com/2009/11/13/mobile-web-design-working-code-tips-best-practices/.

comScore. 2010. "comScore Reports February 2010 U.S. Mobile Subscriber Market Share." Accessed May 25, 2010. http://www.comscore.com/Press_Events/Press_Releases/2010/4/comScore_Reports_February_2010_U.S._Mobile_Subscriber_Market_Share.

Farkas, Meredith. n.d. "Library Success: A Best Practices Wiki Section 'M-Libraries.'" Accessed May 25, 2010. http://www.libsuccess.org/index.php?title=M-Libraries.

Google Code. n.d. "iUI - Project Hosting on Google Code." Accessed May 27, 2010. http://code.google.com/p/iui/.

Index Data. 2008. "PHPYAZ | Index Data." Accessed May 27, 2010. http://www.indexdata.com/phpyaz.

Innovative Interfaces. n.d. "AirPAC: Innovative Interfaces." Accessed May 25, 2010. http://www.iii.com/products/airpac.shtml.

Nielsenwire. 2010. "Smartphones to Overtake Feature Phones in U.S. by 2011." Accessed May 25, 2010. http://blog.nielsen.com/nielsenwire/consumer/smartphones-to-overtake-feature-phones-in-u-s-by-2011/.

North Carolina State University. n.d. "Computer Availability." Accessed May 27, 2010. http://www.lib.ncsu.edu/m/compavail/.

NPD Group. 2010. "Android Shakes Up U.S. Smartphone Market." Accessed May 25, 2010. http://www.npd.com/press/releases/press_100510.html.

Spalding, Tim. 2010. "Library Anywhere, a Mobile Catalog for Everyone." *Thingology Blog*. Accessed May 25, 2010. http://www.librarything.com/blogs/thingology/2010/01/library-anywhere-a-mobile-catalog-for-everyone/.

UNC Libraries. 2009. "UNC Libraries Mobile Website." Accessed May 27, 2010. http://www.lib.unc.edu/m/#_home.

Wisniewski, J. 2010. "Mobile Websites with Minimum Effort." *Online 34* 1: 54–7.

Developing Library Websites Optimized for Mobile Devices

BRENDAN RYAN

Phillips Memorial Library, Providence College, Providence, RI

The article explores the development of library web sites optimized for mobile devices. Topics to be covered will include beginning the process of developing for mobile devices, assessing project goals, text-based contact with library staff, and mobile device emulators.

INTRODUCTION

Mobile devices are becoming a fixture of contemporary life. They are coming to be the primary means for communication and access to the Internet for many people. In light of this situation, anticipating future developments and to meet the needs of the student body, many academic libraries are beginning the project of developing a site optimized for mobile devices.

The primary considerations when designing with mobile devices in mind are in accommodating differing screen-widths, browsers, and processing speeds. An important strategy to address these issues rests in limiting clickstream. Mobile devices do not have as much processing power as personal computers and allowances must be made for this in the design process.

To make the most efficient use of time and effort in this project, it is best to clearly identify the purpose of the site so that it is directed by target goals. In addition, a realistic assessment of institutional competencies and support helps to inform development efforts. An appealing site will help generate use and ensure that development efforts are receptively met.

Perusing the available mobile sites outside of the library community can prove an excellent development strategy.

To satisfy the peculiarities of mobile devices, several coding strategies should be employed. Proportionally sizing text and images to accommodate screen-width variation can be accomplished through the following methods. Visual formatting for mobile devices is important and distinct from design strategies for personal computers. When undertaking the design process, important best practices to be mindful of are the use of CSS and validation services. A profusion of free tools and emulators exists to aid the project.

PRIMARY CONSIDERATIONS WHEN DESIGNING FOR MOBILE DEVICES

Screen sizes present the largest variable in designing for mobile devices. They vary from approximately 120 to 480 pixels in width. Attempting to design with the limitations of each individual screen in mind is not possible. Some efforts have been made to design library sites for specific devices, such as the iPhone app available at the University of Virginia. In the process of outlining goals for a mobile project, this is an issue that should be addressed. In conjunction with screen size, browser variation presents the other major variable in mobile devices.

When taking screen size variation into account, designers should make some accommodations to present sites that are more appealing. Images should be basic and distinct. Because of the small size of screens, it may be difficult to distinguish elements of objects or even objects themselves. In addition, "[m]obile devices are often used outdoors. Glare can wash-out the screen, so think high-contrast for your color scheme" (Wisniewski 2010, 56). Text should also be limited to essential information and be legible. It would not be advisable to present fonts that are not clear. In most cases, users are accessing information through a mobile device for immediate use. They want hours, directions, or other information while on the go (hence the term "mobile device"), so designers should keep that in mind and provide information in the most simple way possible. It is unlikely that users want several lines of text, let alone several pages, to get the information they need. Initial interaction with mobile web sites should be simple while allowing the user to access more content if desired. The effort to distill information on the site will have the benefit of adding usability while also lessening the processing burden on the device. It is important to remember that devices are not as powerful as full-sized computers.

An excellent explication of browser considerations in mobile devices is available in Jeff Wisniewski's article "Mobile Websites With Minimal Effort." He outlines the current state of browser variation in mobile devices by delineating between smartphones and all other mobile devices.

Smartphones have an operating system based on WebKit browsers, such as Safari and those employed in Android phones that represent a Google OS. Smartphones account for "more than 50% of mobile internet traffic" (Wisniewski 2010). Wisniewski outlines a development strategy that is tailored to smartphones while incorporating features that will function on other devices.

It is important to develop coding in CSS that directs mobile devices and smartphones to the proper site. Often, smartphones do not declare themselves to be handheld devices with the term "mobile," ignoring mobile stylesheets. In this case, it is important to develop another stylesheet that directs itself to browsers of a specific screen-width. A strategy to deal with this when designing a mobile site is to employ two style sheets, named simply mobile.css and iphone.css. Those devices that are not directed to the mobile site based on the mobile.css stylesheet will be identified and subject to the iphone.css stylesheet based on screen-width.

Streamlining clickstream is an important factor when developing your site. Clickstream refers to the number of sites one needs to access to get the desired information. Devices are often not well-equipped to navigate through various links. This is particularly important when access keys need to be employed to use a site. This act can be frustrating and time-consuming for the user. As librarians, we want to make products that will facilitate interaction with the library and encourage future use. In addition, cost considerations often can affect a patron's use of the site with a mobile device. If procuring desired information requires access to several pages, it will turn the user off. Pages generally load slowly on mobile devices. Data plan subscribers often incur additional costs when using a service beyond the agreed upon amount. Limiting clickstream not only limits user frustration, but also limits costs to the user, making it more likely the site will be seen as valuable.

PLANNING THE PROCESS

Assess the resources available when beginning development. It is best to clearly understand the possibilities of and constraints on the project. Constraints largely dictate what is possible in the project. In certain cases, an institution will include a large computer studies program with students or faculty that can provide assistance or development support.

Identify a purpose for the project. Does the site aim to provide general information such as hours, directions, and staff directories? Does the institution place a high priority on communication between patrons and staff through mobile devices? Are the catalog or database subscription services things that are important for mobile users to have access to? The purposes of the project should be informed by patron needs or wants.

Identifying the scope and purpose of a mobile site greatly assists in the design effort. Features may be basic, such as general library information like hours and directions, or interactive, such as texting functionality and e-mail forms. Texting is an activity the millennial generation cannot do without, as anyone who spends time in an academic library will tell you.

Texting and e-mailing staff are important features of a mobile site. In colleges and universities that serve many commuter and continuing education students, this presents an excellent way to enhance the learning experience. Certainly, the extension of services to communicate electronically between faculty and students represents an area of exciting possibilities and future growth. To generate a form for e-mailing a librarian, one can use the Email Me Form (http://www.emailmeform.com/). This is an excellent free site that develops forms based on user needs. It is simple to use and presents coding that is valid. You may have to tweak the coding so that it lines up with the coding format specified on the other pages. The use of the Email Me Form provides a correct form, while saving the time and frustration involved in creating forms with HTML.

It is helpful when beginning development to browse other mobile sites. A multiplicity of examples outside of the library field exists, such as the *New York Times*, BBC, and ESPN. Accessing sites with various devices allows you to see what works. Perhaps design or formatting styles that would work well for a library site can be discovered. It is important to remain abreast of developments outside of the academic world that appeal to users. Several fine examples of mobile sites developed for libraries exist. Impressive and informative sites have been created by the New York Public Library (http://m.nypl.org/) and Oregon State University (http://m.library.oregonstate.edu/).

DESIGN FEATURES

To allow text to proportionally format to varying screen-widths, use percentages or ems to size text. Absolute point font sizes will not transfer well to mobile devices. A line of 20 point font text can take up an entire device screen in certain circumstances. This is unsettling. Even if a site does present all the information contained in a page, incorrectly sized text will make the scrolling necessary to access it render text useless on a mobile device. Ems and percentage are malleable values that allow browsers to scale content to fit screens. One em represents a 16 point font on a standard computer browser. Text can be proportionally sized by presenting different em values.

Images are important factors in developing a visually appealing site. It is important to follow a few guidelines in employing images in a mobile site. To ensure images are conspicuous, they should be simple and stark. Images containing gradient colors or a large color pallet may not transfer to mobile devices well. In addition, detailed images generally present a larger file size. One of the ways to minimize file size is to keep images simple. Another tool designers can employ to reduce file size is to provide the images as gifs rather than jpegs. Comparable files saved as a jpeg can be several bytes larger than a gif. A consideration in minimizing load time involves incorporating them into CSS rather than HTML code. This adds consistency to a site while also simplifying the need to make changes. Rather than deal with a slew of individual HTML files to make graphic changes, they can be made by editing a few of the CSS files.

After identifying important image characteristics and file formats, designers will have to deal with the issue of image size. Unlike text, images cannot be sized in ems, so an absolute size must be identified for images used on a site. To ensure consistency in appearance, images should be kept to the same absolute size. Testing a beta version of a mobile site with varying devices can provide guidance regarding image sizing. An excellent source for procuring images was the Open Clipart Library (http://www.openclipart. org/). An array of images is available in an open source community.

Best practice in designing sites for mobile devices is to incorporate all stylistic elements into CSS. Incorporating all of the design elements into stylesheets has several advantages. Of particular importance for mobile devices is the benefit of reducing the size of HTML pages. This will speed up load time and, in turn, lessen costs to users. The use of stylesheets also allows the designer to make global changes to the site easily. It provides a mechanism for creating a uniform look on all pages. Another coding specification when designing for mobile devices is to avoid the use of tables. Due to the varying characteristics presented by mobile devices, the use of tables presents a litany of problems.

The final step in the design process involves validation. Two tools are provided by the W3 School to undertake this, a Validator (http://validator. w3.org/) and mobileOK Checker (http://validator.w3.org/mobile/). The best point to start at is the standard HTML validator. Designers can use this to validate HTML and CSS. It is less demanding than the mobile checker, so adhering to its suggestions will be less exhaustive and set you on the right path. The mobileOK Checker provides more specific evaluation for mobile devices and can take more time to satisfy. It can be intimidating to first approach validation. Initially, a page may display scores of errors, yet often simple fixes remove several errors. Validating all code ensures that a site complies to accepted HTML standards and will appear consistently when accessed with multiple browsers.

TOOLS TO ASSIST IN THE DEVELOPMENT PROCESS

Developing a mobile site with basic HTML text editors is often most effective. Due to the limitations presented by mobile devices relating to screen width, processing speed, and other factors, mobile sites often need to be very simple to function properly. Editors allow the user to work with the design at the most basic level and direct designers toward simple solutions. In addition, the editors outlined in this section are cross-compatible. Documents can be saved as text and transferred between programs.

Notetab Pro (http://www.notetab.com/) is an excellent free text editor. A 30-day trial is provided for this edition. There are three editions of Notetab, with the Light version available as freeware. Although this program is serviceable, it can become difficult to edit documents because it does not provide text line numbers. This necessitates the purchase of the Pro version after the trial period ends.

Code Lobster (http://www.codelobster.com/) is another free editor available for download on the web. There are no distinct disadvantages when compared with Notetab Pro while presenting an obvious cost benefit. Both of these programs only work with the Windows operating system. Workarounds such as Parallels or WINE can be employed to make them function with Apple or Linux operating systems, yet the efficacy of these endeavors is questionable.

OpenOffice.org has developed an editor that is highly functional: Bluefish (http://bluefish.openoffice.nl/). This program is designed to work with Linux operating systems, yet it can be employed on a Mac using the WINE program if the user is savvy enough with applications. In many ways, it is a text editor with some of the features presented by Dreamweaver. Bluefish incorporates HTML wizards, multi-language support, and other features absent from Notetab or Code Lobster while also presenting the same investment.

Dreamweaver is a powerful program but has many disadvantages, particularly when designing for mobile devices. An obvious drawback to working with Dreamweaver is its cost. There are more effective programs available for free. The Adobe Creative Suite does contain excellent and useful programs, such as Photoshop, to allow you to work with images.

Coding in documents created by Dreamweaver can be very sloppy. This is partly related to intrinsic features of the program. The program inserts coding that is superfluous to HTML coding when handling graphics or creating a template. This enables documents to access formatting or images through the use of proprietary code. Although sites created by Dreamweaver can work well, this feature provides an additional level of complexity that is not desirable when designing for mobile devices. File size can become excessive. In addition, the proprietary file formats that Dreamweaver saves in are not cross compatible with other programs. Although Dreamweaver does provide users the option of saving documents in formats that are universal, the code the program develops to links files and pages is not recognized by other programs and is very difficult for the user to manipulate.

Dreamweaver does provide users with a validation feature but it does not create valid code initially. Users can employ this feature throughout the process of design, but even if code is validated through Dreamweaver problems may be present on mobile devices. The proprietary code referred to above can be validated but does present problems. When designing for mobile devices, it is important to design while remaining cognizant of the fact that the processors you are designing for will not be as powerful as those of contemporary desktops.

In light of the previous discussion of browser variation on mobile devices, employing reliable device emulators in the design process is vital. Several options will be presented that should provide an excellent starting point. Mobile devices use a variety of browsers and a coherent set of design standards has yet to be implemented for mobile browsers. Devices profiles vary widely, yet standards seem to be emerging as smartphones become more common.

The Opera browser (http://www.opera.com/), employed by many devices, is readily available for desktop use. This is an effective method for viewing how different designs would appear on devices with varying screen widths. Firefox is employed on some devices, but the desktop version does not account for variations in screen-width. A helpful feature of Firefox is the User-Agent Switcher (https://addons.mozilla.org/en-US/firefox/addon/59/). This add-on allows the user to change the browser characteristics to those of any device. It is installed with an option to act as an iPhone. When selected, sites will appear as they do on an iPhone, even directing your browser to the mobile site in the case where that is in the code of the accessed site. A search of the Internet will allow the user to find the information necessary to add different device profiles to this add-on.

Austrian web-developer Klaus Komenda has developed a site that enables users to view how a site appears on particular devices (http://www.klauskomenda.com/archives/2008/03/17/testing-on-mobile-devices-using-emulators/), allowing designers to view an image of the physical device as well. This is a handy tool because it allows users to fully appreciate how a particular site feels with a particular device.

Dreamweaver provides a device emulation program, but it is not very helpful. The program included with CS4 did not present emulators for many recently developed smartphones. Perhaps this situation has been remedied through recent updates.

Apart from employing emulators, it is helpful to test your site using Internet Explorer. It provides tangible benefits to use different incarnations because devices vary in which version they employ. Unlike Firefox or Opera, Internet Explorer is particular and dated about which code it recognizes. Certain CSS code, such as that which pertains to text-shadowing or rounded button corners, is not recognized. You can chose to eliminate this code from your design or employ a different strategy, such as the one Jeff Wisniewski discusses in relation to smartphones and older mobile devices. Designers can include certain code with the understanding that it will only be recognized on certain devices. If this is accounted for in the design process, certain devices can present different design features on the site.

CONCLUSION

The process of designing a mobile site presents many opportunities to learn and should provide a means for designers to further refine and expand on libraries' mobile offerings. Strategies and tactics that will inform the continued development process should be employed. Contemporary academic libraries that seek to remain abreast of mobile developments counteract the tendency "[a]mong young people. . .to consider the library as primarily the domain of the book" (American Library Association 2007). The incorporation of a mobile site into a library's toolkit enables the institution to better meet the users where they are.

REFERENCES

American Library Association. 2007. "ACRL: Changing Roles of Academic and Research Libraries." Association of College and Research Libraries, February 13. Accessed June 2, 2010. http://www.ala.org/ala/mgrps/divs/acrl/issues/value/changingroles.cfm.
Wisniewski, Jeff. 2010. "Mobile Websites with Minimum Effort." *Online* 34: 54–7.

Smartphones, Smart Objects, and Augmented Reality

HARRY E. PENCE

State University of New York College at Oneonta, Oneonta, NY

Two major types of augmented reality seem most likely to see academic use in the coming five years, markerless and marked. Markerless augmented reality uses the location determined by a cell phone to serve as a basis for adding local information to the camera view. Marked augmented reality uses a two-dimensional barcode to connect a cell phone or personal computer to information, usually on a web site. Both approaches are already being used in museums and college libraries. Marked augmented reality is especially powerful because it makes physical objects clickable, such as a web page. Augmented reality creates some exciting new opportunities for libraries.

INTRODUCTION

Faculty attitudes toward the cell phone have been mixed, to say the least. For a sampling of opinions on both sides, read the Slashdot blog that contains comments about a professor who decided to eliminate student cell phone use in his classroom by disconnecting the WiFi connection (Story 2003). It is unfortunate that many academics wish to ban cell phones from their classes because the modern cell phone (often called a smartphone) can be a powerful tool for education.

The author wishes to acknowledge the inspiration and support of Lori Bell, who continues to be a leader in library innovation.

The smartphone is the Swiss Army knife of modern communications. It combines a telephone with a global positioning system (GPS), a camera, a compass, an accelerometer, WiFi support, and a web browser. These features allow the device to determine where it is located and which direction it is pointing and to browse the World Wide Web for content, including streaming video. In addition, there are more than 200,000 free or inexpensive applications (apps) available at the iPhone store, and a rapidly expanding pool of apps for other smartphones. According to a ChangeWave study, 42% of U.S. consumers reported having a smartphone in December 2009, and this value has been increasing rapidly for some time (eMarketer: Digital Intellegence 2010).

Kolb (2008) wrote that there is a disconnect between how students learn outside of school and how they learn in the classroom, and teachers have little appreciation for the skills that students use outside of the classroom. Teachers tend to think of devices such as cell phones as "toys" and see these technologies as distracting and even harmful. One survey suggests that 85% of professors would like to ban cell phones from the classroom. Kolb urges teachers to find ways to integrate cell phones into the classroom. The combination of the cell phone with augmented reality is a prime candidate for this type of integration.

SMARTPHONES AND AUGMENTED REALITY

Augmented (or virtual) reality has been discussed since the late 1960s, but formerly it was considered to be too expensive and cumbersome to be useful (Pausch, Proffitt, and Williams 1997). Only now is it emerging as an important application for communications, research, industry, and art, especially in combination with the smartphone. One of the most commonly seen examples of augmented reality is the "virtual first and 10 line" often seen on television broadcasts of U.S. football games.

There does not seem to be a widely accepted definition of augmented reality (Bimber and Raskar 2005). Milgram and Kishino (1994) described what has come to be known as Milgram's Virtuality Continuum, going from face-to-face contact to digitally enriched environments (such as Heads-up Displays) to physical worlds that are digitally enhanced (such as digital maps) and finally to virtual worlds (such as Second Life). Thus, augmented reality would be a computer-generated component that is added to the real environment, whereas in true virtual reality, the entire experience is computer generated. Perhaps the simplest definition is that Augmented reality is the combination of digital information with the real world.

Although virtual worlds, such as Second Life, have become rather popular for education (Pence 2007–8), it seems probable that augmented reality will affect higher education sooner and more profoundly than virtual worlds. Virtual worlds have the potential to create a far more immersive experience than augmented reality, but many people are uncomfortable with virtual worlds, perhaps because of that realism. Augmented reality literally may provide the best of both worlds.

One current application of augmented reality is the use of Heads-up Displays (HUDs) inside modern aircraft cockpits (Jean 2010). Computer-generated navigational information is projected onto a translucent screen in front of the pilot so it is not necessary to look down at the control panel. Military uses of HUDs are a major factor in accelerating the development of augmented reality applications. For more than a decade, the U.S. military has worked toward linking every vehicle and soldier on the battlefield into a single intranet to improve communications. One component of this system, the U.S. Army's Land Warrior System for the combat infantryman, includes a monocle viewer, camera, GPS, and digital radios, all inside the helmet. Apparently, the soldiers consider this eight pound unit to be too heavy, so Defense Advanced Research Projects Agency (DARPA) is hoping to develop a contact lens system with many of the same capabilities (Shachtman 2009).

The 2010 Horizon Report predicts that "augmented reality has become simple, and is now poised to enter the mainstream in the consumer sector" (Johnson et al. 2010). The two main types of cell phone augmented reality currently in use are called markerless, which uses position data from the telephone or image recognition to identify a location and then overlays digital information, in contrast to marker-based, which requires a specific label, such as a bar code, to identify a location. The modern cell phone makes these types of applications available inexpensively and conveniently. An application called Google Goggles can be downloaded for the iPhone, BlackBerry, and Android phones. It is basically a visible search engine that will use a cell phone photograph to deliver information to that telephone about a landmark, tourist location, store, or even a bottle of wine.

Several companies, including Layar, Wikitude, and Junaio, have created markerless augmented reality applets for smartphones. For example, an application created by Layar allows a software developer to overlay information on the video on the phone, combining real life views with digital data. Thus, if someone takes a video of a famous location with their cell phone, the Layer software adds further information on the live camera feed. This creates a new type of guided tourism. Currently, Layar offers up to 87 layers of location-related content, including the location of nearby schools, museums, restaurants, transportation, and health care (Layar, http://www.layar.com).

A similar example has been created by the iTacitus Consortium, with representatives from six different organizations in four European countries. The Consortium explored ways in which information technology could be used to encourage cultural tourism (http://www.itacitus.org/). Intelligent Tourism And Cultural Information Through Ubiquitous Services (iTacitus) uses augmented reality to enhance the experience at cultural heritage sites by adding three-dimensional objects, such as missing paintings or statues, background information as an overlay of the image, or special audio clips appropriate to the location. Based on the interests expressed by the viewer, the iTacitus software can recommend places or events to visit nearby. *Science Daily* calls it a virtual time machine, but Bruce Sterling complains that "soon we'll have some themepark Creationist Augmented Reality, where you can visit the Grand Canyon and see pre-Noachian people pan-frying trilobites and riding dinosaurs" (ScienceDaily 2009).

There are several other location-based cell phone applications. Yelp, which is available on iPhone, BlackBerry, or Android cell phones, asks users to review restaurants, stores, and shopping areas near their location. These ratings are combined to produce a rating of the local businesses, which a later user will see as a layer on his or her photographs. Wikitude allows individual users to customize the viewer experience by adding URLs, phone numbers, or addresses to each point of interest, sometimes called geotagging (http://wikitude.me). Other popular location-based apps include Foursquare, Loopt, and Gowalla (Miller 2010). One of the most popular apps of this type is Foursquare, which allows users to obtain points when "checking in" at a given location, such as a restaurant or movie. Checking in at a location often enough can even earn the designation as "mayor" of the site (until another user checks into the site more frequently).

Several college libraries are already using this type of location-based function to enhance the campus experience. North Carolina State University has created an application called Wolfwalk, which overlays historical images from the library archives at more than 50 major sites of interest on the campus. According to the web site, "an iPhone native app version of WolfWalk is complete and should go live in the Apple App Store in the Summer of 2010" (North Carolina State University Libraries 2010). The Oregon State University Libraries have created a similar smartphone tour (Oregon State University Libraries 2010). A consortium of researchers from Harvard University, the University of Wisconsin at Madison, and MIT have developed a geolocation-based game to teach math and science literacy skills (O'Shea 2010). The game uses Dell Axim handheld computers to allow middle-school students to interact with digital objects and virtual people who exist in an augmented reality world superimposed on a real playground or sports field.

It might appear that the small size of a cell phone screen would make it inconvenient for viewing video applications, but a recent survey indicates that cell phones are increasingly being used for text, web browsing, games, and even watching television (Wortham 2010). Murray (2008) has previously commented that even though the iPhone's display is only 3.5-inches, it is still very usable for routine reference library work. Although relatively few colleges and universities are using this form of augmented reality thus far, the popularity of games (such as FourSquare) with the general public suggests that the small screen size is not a significant constraint for educational use.

SMARTPHONES AND SMART OBJECTS

Probably the simplest form of augmented reality to implement is called marker based because it requires that a camera receive a specific visual cue that allows software to access the desired information. A label can be placed on a physical object that would represent the URL for a web site related to the object. This creates what are called smart objects or intelligent objects. One advantage of online material is that you can power browse from site to site using hyperlinks. Material on ordinary paper that includes a two-dimensional bar code can connect to digital information on the web. Thus, two-dimensional (2D) barcodes make objects in the real world clickable somewhat like a web page.

A number of recent studies suggest that hyperlinks are changing the way that people read. For example, a recent study (Rowlands and Fieldhouse 2007) about the way that researchers of today search for information says "less time is being spent on reading, per article, and researchers 'see' an increasingly narrow view of their own discipline as a result of the growth in the literature." Although some authors view this development with alarm, it seems likely that the convenience of reading this way will outweigh any predictions of doom (Carr 2010).

The linear or 1D (1 dimensional) barcode is now commonly found on almost every product in a store and is shown on the left in Figure 1. It is a way to represent product identification number by the widths and spacings of a set of parallel lines. The number of possible variations in the symbol is relatively small, so it represents only a few digits, although it can link to a database for more information. The 2D bar code (shown on the right in Figure 1) consists of a more complicated pattern of squares, dots, hexagons, or other geometric patterns. Currently, the most common coding pattern

FIGURE 1 One-dimensional bar code (left) and two-dimensional barcode (right).

is called quick response (QR) code. QR code was first used in Japan in 1994, and it is just beginning to be used in the United States. Unlike the one-dimensional bar code, a 2D bar code can represent several thousand characters, more than enough to stand for the URL of a web site.

The November 2009 issue of *Esquire* has several advertisements that contain 2D barcodes (http://www.esquire.com/the-side/augmented-reality). Downloading the special software (Windows and Mac Only) allows the user to hold the barcode up to the computer web cam and connect to a video, web site, or other information. This provides an example of what might be possible, but it has application far beyond a single magazine or software. There seem to be several free online sites available that allow an individual to create 2D bar codes for web site addresses (IDAutomation, http://www.bcgen.com/datamatrix-barcode-creator.html), and some iPhone apps, like 2DSense, can open a web link from the bar code. Microsoft has created its own tagging system (in color) that creates tags, and Microsoft also provide a free smartphone app to read the tags (Microsoft 2010).

On a college campus, this technique might be used for something as simple as labeling various campus locations or creating easily accessible supplemental material about the exhibits in a museum. An interactive gallery or museum exhibit with a QR code could allow a patron to access a web site or an audio lecture about the object. Stetson University is using undergraduate students to develop this type of program (Stetson University 2009). A wiki is available that provides numerous examples of the application of augmented reality to education (Hamilton 2010). Other possibilities include adding a barcode with laboratory directions to a syllabus, which will then connect to a video web site that contains further information.

Several libraries are already using 2D QR barcodes. The blog Bibliothekia suggests that it will be possible to set up QR codes for different sections of a collection so that patrons could be informed any time a new book is added to that section. The same blog quotes Nate Hill, from The Brooklyn Public Library, who proposes that every book should have its own web page ("QR Codes and Libraries" 2008). Phillips Memorial Library at Providence College is using QR coded tags to provide directions to a collection or a department, play tutorial videos, and offer support contact information (Pulliam and Landry 2010). According to a recent note in *The Library Journal,* Contra Costa County Library, CA is attaching QR symbols to library-related materials and placing them in high-traffic areas to connect patrons with library services (Hadro 2010). The ReadWriteWeb Blog suggests some other ways to use QR codes (Perez 2008).

The QR Cloud Project in Amsterdam, the Netherlands, is an example that uses QR codes to present stories, poems, and proverbs written by Dutch writers, poets, and scientists that are short enough to code on a single barcode (Beekmans 2009). Some publishers are putting 2D barcodes on their books to connect readers to a site with reviews and ordering information. For more information, including other sites for creating or reading QR barcodes, the QR 2D online magazine is an excellent source (Smolski 2010).

THE FUTURE OF AUGMENTED REALITY

There are several indications that the future of augmented reality for general use seems bright. The geolocation application called FourSquare already has over 350,000 users and is still growing (Beaumont 2010). A color 2D coding system, called Mobile Multi-Colour Composite (MMCC), is under development that can store more information, enough to encode whole songs and other information (Wilson 2009). It has enough information storage capacity that connection to the Internet or other source may no longer be necessary.

Applications of augmented reality in higher education are not yet widespread but, as noted above, seem to be becoming increasingly popular in libraries and museums. There is a recent rumor that Facebook will soon support the use of 2D QR barcodes for users, and if this is true it would represent a major development (Wauters 2010). Although many academics are hesitant to accept any application based on cell phones in class, widespread adoption by young people would make it more difficult for higher education to resist.

One of the main limitations on the current systems is the need for an improved cell phone screen display. The current smartphone is very convenient for carrying, but rather small for prolonged viewing. Hainich (2006) argued that an operating system should show objects in the three-dimensional (3D) space of the real world rather than on the traditional 2D screen. He wrote that "the next logical step is to pull these devices and objects from the computer screen back into the real world and use our entire environment as a giant 3D screen." The HUDs that are being investigated for the military applications suggest that this idea is not something from science fiction.

If a HUD can be incorporated into a pair of glasses, it can create a book that is truly a smart object. An architecture student named Sorin Voicu from the Valle Giulia faculty of Architecture in Italy has visualized this possibility in a video that he created as his thesis project. When a book is viewed through these special glasses, virtual tabs appear on the book, which allow the reader to manipulate the illustrations, run a movie, or even convert a floor plan into a 3D image. This level of interaction is not yet available commercially, but it will certainly create new educational possibilities when it is.

It seems safe to assume that as augmented reality applications become more widely accepted the technology will develop more rapidly. Parviz (2009) stated that ". . . a contact lens with simple built-in electronics is already within reach." Predictions about future technologies are often overly optimistic, but this discussion at least suggests that it may be possible in the foreseeable future to replace even the HUDs that are being discussed today in favor of contact lenses that will provide the same functionality. The lens would contain optoelectronics that will display augmented reality information while remaining semitransparent so that the user will see a data field overlaid on his or her vision of the real world. Initially, such a lens might show only a few pixels of information, but even this could be useful. The ultimate experience would be to access the Internet and provide a constant flow of data about the surrounding environment.

CONCLUSION

Augmented reality offers many advantages for education. It expands the usefulness of the cell phone, a device that is already very popular with students and the general public. A marker-based program can be developed for minimal cost, which is an important consideration at a time when finances are so tight for all types of institutions. The breadth of the program can be adjusted based on available staff time. Such a program lends itself to being phased in over a period of time or deployed all at once. It provides new connections between the public and the archives and other collections that already exist at many libraries and museums. Augmented reality offers many new opportunities for innovation and meshes well with the current public interest in social networks. Perhaps most important, it builds on the natural curiosity of the students and the public, so it is more about individual learning than restricted programs or courses.

As early as 2004, Alexander (2004) pointed out that "the combination of wireless technology and mobile computing is resulting in escalating transformations of the educational world." He predicted that mobile devices will make the information and communications power of the Internet available without regard to time or location, creating what he called mobile learning, or m-learning. The combination of smartphones with powerful and inexpensive augmented reality applications makes his prediction especially relevant.

REFERENCES

Alexander, Bryan. 2004. "Going Nomadic: Mobile Learning in Higher Education." *EDUCAUSE Review* 39(5): 28–35.

Beaumont, Claudine. 2010. "Foursquare Enjoys Surge of Popularity." *The Daily Telegraph*. Accessed June 3, 2010. http://www.telegraph.co.uk/technology/social-media/7165699/Foursquare-enjoys-surge-of-popularity.html.

Beekmans, Joroen. 2009. "The QR Cloud Project: Micro Secrets in Public Space." *The Pop-Up City*, September 28. Accessed June 3, 2010. http://popupcity.net/2009/09/the-qr-cloud-project-micro-secrets-in-public-space/.

Bimber, Olver, and Ramesh Raskar. 2005. *Spatial Augmented Reality: Merging Real and Virtual Worlds: 2*. Natick, MA: A. K. Peters, Ltd.

Carr, Nicholas. 2010. *The Shallows: What the Internet is Doing to Our Brains*. New York: W. W. Norton & Company.

eMarketer: Digitial Intelligence. 2010. "Android Surges among Handset Purchasers." Accessed May 5, 2010. http://www.emarketer.com/Article.aspx?R=1007462.

Hadro, Josh. 2010. "QR Codes to Extend Library's Reach in Contra Costa." Accessed June 9, 2010. http://www.libraryjournal.com/lj/technologylibrary20/853479-295/qr_codes_to_extend_libraryaposs.html.csp.

Hainich, Rolf R. 2006. *The End of Hardware: A Novel Approach to Augmented Reality, 2nd edition*: Booksurge LLC.

Hamilton, Karen E. 2010. "Augmented Reality in Education." Accessed May 15, 2010. http://wik.ed.uiuc.edu/index.php/Augmented_Reality_in_Education#Augmented_Reality:_In_Everyday_Life.

Jean, Grace V. 2010. "Taking 'Heads-Up' Displays to the Next Level." *National Defense Magazine*, March 2010. Accessed May 13, 2010. http://www.nationaldefensemagazine.org/archive/2010/March/Pages/HeadsUpDisplays.aspx.

Johnson, L., A. Levine, R. Smith, and S. Stone. 2010. "The 2010 Horizon Report." Accessed June 2, 2010. http://www.nmc.org/pdf/2010-Horizon-Report.pdf.

Kolb, Liz. 2008. *Toys to Tools: Connecting Student Cell Phones to Education*. Eugene, OR: International Society for Teaching in Education.

Microsoft. 2010. "Connecting Real Life and the Digital World." Accessed June 3, 2010. http://tag.microsoft.com/consumer/index.aspx.

Milgram, P., and F. A. Kishino. 1994. Taxonomy of Mixed Reality Visual Displays. *IECE Trans on Information and Systems* E77-D: 1321–9.

Miller, Claire Cain. 2010. "Cell Phone in a New Role: Loyalty Card." *New York Times*, June 1, 2010, B1.

Murray, David C. 2008. "iReference: Using Apple's iPhone as a Reference Tool." *The Reference Librarian* 49: 167–70.

North Carolina State University Libraries. 2010. "WolfWalk." Accessed June 8, 2010. http://www.lib.ncsu.edu/dli/projects/wolfwalk/.

O'Shea, Patrick. 2010. "Handheld Augmented Reality Project (HARP)." Accessed June 9, 2010. http://isites.harvard.edu/icb/icb.do?keyword=harp&pageid=icb.page69587.

Oregon State University Libraries. 2010. "OSU History Goes Mobile." Accessed June 8, 2010. http://osulibrary.oregonstate.edu/beavertracks.

Parviz, Babak A. 2009. "Augmented Reality in a Contact Lens." Accessed May 29, 2010. http://spectrum.ieee.org/biomedical/bionics/augmented-reality-in-a-contact-lens/0.

Pausch, Randy, Dennis Proffitt, and George Williams. 1997. "Quantifying Immersion in Virtual Reality." Accessed May 14, 2010. http://www.cs.cmu.edu/~stage3/publications/97/conferences/siggraph/immersion/.

Pence, Harry E. 2007-8. "The Homeless Professor in Second Life." *Journal of Education Technology Systems* 36: 171–7.

Perez, Sarah. 2008. "The Scannable World, Part 3: Barcode Scanning in the Real World." *ReadWriteWeb*, September 26. Accessed June 9, 2010. http://www.

readwriteweb.com/archives/the_scannable_world_barcodes_scanning_in_the_real_world.php.

Pulliam, B., and C. Landry 2010. "QR in the Library." Accessed June 9, 2010. http://providence.libguides.com/content.php?pid=76255&sid=565728.

"QR Codes and Libraries." 2008. *Bibliothekia.* Accessed June 9, 2010. http://bibliothekia.blogspot.com/2008/09/qr-codes-and-libraries.html.

Rowlands, I., and M. Fieldhouse. 2007. "Trends in Scholarly Information Behavior: Work Package I." Accessed December 4, 2010. http://www.ucl.ac.uk/infostudies/research/ciber/downloads/GG%20Work%20Package%20I.pdf.

ScienceDaily. 2009. "Visual Time Machine Offers Tourists a Glimpse of the Past." *ScienceDaily,* August 17. Accessed May 15, 2010. http://www.sciencedaily.com/releases/2009/08/090812104219.htm.

Shachtman, N. 2009. "The Army's New Land Warrior Gear: Why Soldiers Don't Like It." *Popular Mechanics,* October 1. Accessed May 5, 2010. http://www.popularmechanics.com/technology/military/4215715.

Smolski, R. 2010. "Around the World in 80 Days with QR Codes." *2d Code*, May 28. Accessed June 9, 2010. http://2d-code.co.uk/around-the-world-with-qr-codes/.

Stetson University. 2009. "At Stetson, Sophomores Write Real-World Apps." Accessed May 15, 2010. https://www.stetson.edu/secure/apps/wordpress/?p=4981.

Story, Emma. 2003. "Lecture Hall Back-Channeling." *slashdot*, July 24. Accessed May 5, 2010. http://science.slashdot.org/articles/03/07/24/1347242.shtml?tid=146&tid=99.

Wauters, Robin. 2010. "Facebook Kicks Off Implementation of QR Codes." *TechCrunch,* May 16. Accessed June 4, 2010. http://techcrunch.com/2010/03/16/facebook-qr-code/.

Wilson, Mark. 2009. "Barcodes Can Now Hold Entire Videos and Games." *Gizmodo,* March 16. Accessed June 4, 2010. http://gizmodo.com/5170695/barcodes-can-now-hold-entire-videos-and-games.

Wortham, Jenna. 2010. "Cellphones Now Used More for Data than for Calls." *New York Times*, May 13, 2010, B1.

Making Twitter Work: A Guide for the Uninitiated, the Skeptical, and the Pragmatic

VALERIE FORRESTAL

S. C. Williams Library, Stevens Institute of Technology, Hoboken, NJ

This article highlights the advantages of librarians and libraries establishing a professional or institutional presence on Twitter. This basic introduction to the web service also discusses innovative ways to shape your Twitter account into a successful professional development, reference, and outreach resource.

Regardless of what enthusiasts and detractors touting Twitter's boom or doom may say, the service continues to grow at a steady pace (Weil 2010). According to a recent Pew Internet study, one in five internet users is now using online status updating services, such as Twitter (Fox et al. 2009). However, despite its popularity, many continue to poke fun at the rampant "navel-gazing" and banal status updates, such as the oft-cited "what I had for breakfast" posts (Johnson 2009).

How have so many in the library community found value in such a mundane application? The answer may lie in sheer numbers. As of summer 2010, the Twitter directories WeFollow and Twellow list 996 and 7,977 librarians using Twitter, respectively (http://wefollow.com/twitter/librarian & http://www.twellow.com/category_users/cat_id/1059), and one estimate places the number of library Twitter accounts at approximately 830 (Brown 2010). These numbers are rough at best, but even conservative estimates of the activity of librarians and libraries on Twitter make the time investment worthwhile. In fact, the author of a recent study on measuring influence on Twitter cited an unnamed librarian as being one of the most influential non-celebrity users on the service (Young 2010).

So, what is Twitter and how does it work? In brief terms, Twitter allows you to post short status updates (up to 140 characters each post, including spaces) online. People will follow, or subscribe to, your content to see your posts, called "tweets." Likewise, you can follow other people's accounts to see their updates. Your account can be public (viewable to anyone on the internet) or private (users must request your permission to view your updates).

To talk to, mention, or reference a specific user, you would use the "@" symbol followed by the desired username (e.g., @val_forrestal) within the tweet. If you tweet something that another user finds interesting or useful, he or she can retweet it by placing an "RT" along with a reference to the original poster in front of the original tweet.

Finally, you can use a hashtag, or the "#" symbol, to tag a post with specific keywords. Often events will have a preordained hashtag so that users attending the event can find each other's tweets and those not attending can follow along from another location.

There are plenty of ways to access Twitter: through the Twitter.com web site or using desktop applications, such as TweetDeck or Seesmic. Twitter also has a mobile application (which also works on the iPad) that allows you to sign into several accounts at once, making it easy to switch between personal and institutional accounts. The mobile client also makes attaching pictures and video to your tweets simple and allows for quick URL shortening for long Internet addresses, which can quickly consume your 140 character limit.

If you do not have a smartphone, you can use short message service (SMS; or text messaging) to send and receive messages. You can consult Twitter's *Help Center* for more information on setting up your phone to use the service, either through their mobile web site, app, or SMS/text messaging (http://www.support.twitter.com/articles/14014-twitter-phone-faqs).

Whether tweeting from your personal account or your library's, the most important factor in creating a meaningful and useful experience is to realize that the service provides the means for conversation not just broadcasting. Even your most ordinary tweets can connect you with others within your community if a conversation builds around them. In this spirit, get comfortable with just jumping right in. Talk to people you do not know; respond to their updates if they interest you; or retweet posts that you think will be useful or interesting to your followers. The worst that can happen is that you will be ignored, but in general people use Twitter for the interaction and they enjoy it.

Another tip for creating engagement within Twitter, especially for library or institutional accounts, is to create RSS feeds for certain searches. Even if you don't know what an RSS feed is, this is quite easy to do. Just go to

Twitter's search interface (http://search.twitter.com) and do a search for the name of your library, then click the "feed for this query" link. You can also search for a keyword mentioned within a vicinity of your location. (Use the advanced search for these more complex queries.) If you do not want to use an RSS feed reader (such as Google Reader) to view your search results, there are many services that will send you an e-mail update to alert you when your keywords are mentioned (TweetAlarm, Twilert, and tweetbeep are just a few).

Twitter search alerts essentially allow you to use Twitter as a "proactive" reference tool. For example, you can be notified if someone uses the terms "research," "paper," or "writing" on Twitter within a mile of your location, giving you an opportunity to respond to the poster with research options at your library even if the user does not mention the word "library." With that information, you can reach out to potential library users, who many not even know where to look for assistance, and establish a connection that will bring them in your door (or to your resources).

You can also use search alerts as a "virtual comment box" by giving you a way to actively monitor what people are saying about your library and address their concerns personally. In this capacity, Twitter can be tapped for user feedback and can lead to "thinking-out-of-the-box" ideas for new services or resources.

Speaking of RSS feeds, although Twitter use is increasing, there are many people who do not use the service. You can still reach these people by creating an RSS feed of your updates and publishing it on your web site, your blog, or even your online or e-mail newsletter. There are also services (such as Yakket and Ping) that allow you to automatically send your Twitter updates to your library's Facebook page. These tools allow you to use Twitter to get updates out to your community quickly and easily without the necessity of creating a longer blog post about them.

Twitter's mobile app and SMS service also mean that it is much easier to send out updates from anywhere at any time, so you can pass along pertinent information as it comes along, not just during business hours.

Overall, Twitter is a great way to remind people about events and services, pass along important announcements, as well as to share information that might be only tangentially related to you or your library (such as information from a publisher or a group within your community). In fact, using Twitter to reiterate or amplify the voices in your greater community (by retweeting them or just helping promote their events or concerns through your Twitter account) breeds goodwill toward you and your library.

One particularly innovative use of Twitter by a library is Harvard Library Innovation Laboratory's project, "Library Hose," which generates a tweet every time someone checks out a book from any of their branch libraries and aggregates them to a webpage (http://librarylab.law.harvard.edu/twitter/). Although just an experimental project (which was temporarily suspended as of September 15, 2010), it served as an interesting way to show just how popular and vital Harvard University's libraries are.

Another tip for making the best use of your Twitter presence, especially if it is an institutional one, is to have a strategy in place before diving in (Grabowska 2010):

- Think about the purpose of your account and what you would like to focus on.
- Make sure to have a picture, a bio, and a link to your web site, if available, for credibility (that goes for both personal and library accounts).
- Make sure the appearance of your page matches with your overall branding scheme by using your logo and official colors.

For official accounts, you should also have a best practices guide which outlines your purposes and goals, and general rules for behavior and inter-action. A great starting point is Brian Solis' (2010) recent post on the social media blog, Mashable, which sets out 21 "rules of engagement" for any social media campaign or presence. One of his notable points recommends moving beyond marketing into becoming a real participant in your online community. It is extremely important to foster conversation and interaction and to listen and react to your users' concerns and needs. Doing so not only breeds trust, but also inspires advocacy on your part, something of which today's libraries are in dire need.

There are also several good library-specific social media best practices and policy guides that you can use as a starting point for your institution. Posted recently on the blogs, *Tame the Web* and *Librarians Matter*, they rec-ommend being honest, professional, conversational, helpful, and respectful (Greenhill and Fay 2010). They also warn that, although you should aim to be as transparent and open as possible, you should be careful not to divulge confidential information (Stephens 2010). Probably the most important rule with any institutional social media account is to check it regularly, especially if you are using it in a reference capacity. Users will quickly grow frustrated with an organization that ignores their questions and concerns, even if they suspect you are not intentionally doing so. Libraries implementing these types of services should have a point person who is held responsible for regularly checking and updating the accounts, even if several people have access to them (Murphy 2010).

Finally, a story: when I first started my library's Twitter account, I took a lot of flak about it. Some people at my institution felt that I was wasting work time on a purely recreational and narcissistic medium. Then, one day a Twitter search that I had set up as an RSS feed alerted me that someone had mentioned my place of work in a tweet. A graduating student complained that his school e-mail account, which kept him informed on news and events relating to the school, was being disconnected. I responded to this student on Twitter, sending him a list of the school's Twitter accounts and Facebook pages. The student was pleased and wrote a blog post about this experience. I then took the time to comment on his post, thanking him for writing about us.

This story taught me a few lessons about Twitter's potential value in my community. One is that students are more likely to donate and be active alumni if they have methods of easily maintaining a tie to the school. Another is that Twitter can act as a starting point for greater conversation. If it sparks an interaction, you should be willing to take that interaction to other places the user may be. If you direct them to a Facebook page or blog, continue the conversation there. If they are more comfortable moving the conversation to e-mail or the phone, be accommodating.

Twitter is invaluable for creating a network of colleagues who connect me not only to other people of relevance to me, but also to relevant information, events, breaking news, and professional development resources. This network is almost always responsive and available to bounce ideas off of, get the word out, and even answer reference questions. They allow me vicariously to attend conferences and workshops that I cannot attend in person and expose me to sources and viewpoints that I would not have encountered on my own. This community of active professionals, and the ongoing conversations that surround them, brings vitality to the profession that can only serve to keep the field relevant and vibrant, acting as a catalyst to advance libraries into the future.

REFERENCES

Brown, Lindy. 2010. "Libraries on Twitter (Updated List)." *Circulation*, September 19. Accessed September 21, 2010. http://lindybrown.com/blog/2009/01/libraries-on-twitter-updated-list/.

Fox, Susannah, Kathryn Zickuhr, and Aaron Smith. 2009. "Twitter and Status Updating, Fall 2009." Pew Internet & American Life Project, October 21. Accessed June 1, 2010. http://www.pewinternet.org/Reports/2009/17-Twitter-and-Status-Updating-Fall-2009.aspx?r=1.

Grabowska, Kasia. 2010. "Social Media Best Practices for Libraries: A TTW Guest Post." *Tame The Web*, March 18. Accessed September 16, 2010. http://tametheweb.com/2010/03/18/social-media-best-practices-for-libraries/.

Greenhill, Kathryn, and Jean Hing Fay. 2010. "A Social Media Policy for a One Branch Public Library." *Librarians Matter*, September 10. Accessed September 16, 2010. http://librariansmatter.com/blog/2010/09/10/a-social-media-policy-for-a-one-branch-public-library/.

Johnson, Steven. 2009. "How Twitter Will Change the Way We Live." *Time*, June 5. Accessed June 1, 2010. http://www.time.com/time/business/article/0,8599,1902604,00.html.

Murphy, Joe. 2010. "Management Models and Considerations for Virtual Reference." *Science & Technology Libraries* 29: 176. doi:10.1080/01942620802205579.

Solis, Brian. 2010. "21 Rules for Social Media Engagement." *Mashable, The Social Media Guide*, May 18. Accessed June 1, 2010. http://mashable.com/2010/05/18/rules-social-media-engagment/.

Stephens, Michael. 2010. "Anytown Public Library's Social Media Policy." *Tame The Web*, June 10. Accessed September 16, 2010.http://tametheweb.com/2010/06/10/anytown-public-librarys-social-media-policy/.

Weil, Kevin. 2010. "Measuring Tweets." *Twitter Blog,* February 22. Accessed June 1, 2010. http://blog.twitter.com/2010/02/measuring-tweets.html.

Young, Jeff. 2010. "Researchers Find 'Million-Follower Fallacy' in Twitter." *The Chronicle of Higher Education. Wired Campus,* May 25. Accessed June 1, 2010. http://chronicle.com/blogPost/Researchers-Find/24290/.

SMS Reference

SIAN BRANNON

Denton Public Library, Denton, TX

Reference service is evolving. Face-to-face, e-mail, or virtual service—it seems the possibility is endless. A recent trend is to conduct reference interviews through short message service on cell phones. This article looks at why, how, and who is doing it.

REFERENCE VIA SEMAPHORE?

The practice of reference has existed as long as libraries have been around, but the method of answering queries has evolved. Traditional reference work is done between two parties: one with a research need and the other with the knowledge of sources to help ascertain an answer or gather research. From the first research libraries to recent ones, this encounter almost always occurred between two parties meeting face-to-face. Although it is amusing to think of early American settlers conducting reference transactions via smoke signals or by the telegraph or even by semaphores, it seems more likely that the two parties involved were communicating while standing immediately in front of each other.

After the Pony Express belong, it theoretically became possible for someone to "mail" a query across the land if they were patient enough to wait for a response. When libraries installed telephones in their buildings, the length of wait-time for a response became shorter. It also allowed for customers to conduct their reference transactions in real time while remaining in their homes. This is a huge boon to convenience for the customer and is a great customer service.

In the mid-1990s when the Internet began being used in libraries, many reference departments made use of email as a new outlet for conducting reference transactions. Online technologies evolved, and the concept of e-mail combined with phone transactions led to instant messaging. With instant messaging, customers could now "talk" to a librarian through their computer in real-time. "Virtual reference," as it is also known, is an improvement over phone conversations and e-mail because it allows for two-way conversation and the sharing of online resources.

What else can there be? Well, computers and online technologies are not the only devices that have evolved. Phones have gone from rotary to push button, corded to cordless, and landline to mobile. Mobile phones have evolved even further, with their primary functions not necessarily being traditional "phone calls." Now, users can e-mail, surf the Internet, shop, play games, and send text messages to hundreds of their closest friends.

MOBILE GENERATION

According to the 2008 "Future of the Internet III" report published by the Pew Internet & American Life Project, technology stakeholders believe that the mobile phone (or device) will be the primary connection tool to the Internet for most people in the world in the next ten years (Rainie and Anderson 2008). CTIA The Wireless Association reports that as of December of 2008, 87% of the United States population had wireless telecommunications access and that annually, at least one trillion short message service (SMS) messages are sent (CTIA 2009). Three years prior, the United States only had 69% of the population with mobile devices, and only 81 billion messages were sent annually. They also show that at least 17 out of 100 households only have telephone access on mobile devices, and no traditional land-lines at all.

The Pew Project also reports that experts agree that today's wireless phones will shrink in size but expand in capabilities. It will be more like a multipurpose personal computer than a phone and will be used less for voice communication than for other tasks. One respondent said that it will be more difficult to distinguish between a mobile phone and a laptop. They will become one and the same.

The Pew Project also conducted an extensive survey in December of 2008 of American adults who use the Internet. They asked what types of activities these adults performed online. What they are doing online are things that librarians can help them with:

- 83% look for information on a hobby or interest.
- 75% look for health or medical information.
- 54% look up phones numbers and addresses.
- 47% get sports scores and information.
- 80% check the weather.
- 86% look for driving directions.
- 89% use a search engine to find information.

Knowing that this type of search is what our users are doing, we can help them. If they ask these questions of the library through an easy reference by SMS, they'll receive accurate information from a reliable source, right?

HOW IT WORKS

SMS is a service for communication that usually occurs between mobile telephones. Methods vary depending on the mobile phone model, but most of the time users create a message using the number pad or QWERTY keyboard on their mobile phone, select a destination phone number to which to send the message, and then send it. Most mobile carriers allow between 140 and 160 characters to be used in any one SMS message. Most also allow "concatenation," which connects a series of messages together to be sent, received, and read as either one message or a series of shorter parts.

Some libraries use keyword queries, which involve having users start their text message with a specific term, such as "address," to get canned responses about library locations. Another example is "program" to find out what is happening at the library, or "reference" to direct their queries to an appropriate department. Use of these keyword query-starters provides for additional outlets for program promotion, marketing, and information delivery.

MAJOR LIBRARY VENDORS

Altarama (www.altarama.com)

Although it started as an Australian company, Altarama provided the platform for the first United States text messaging reference service at Southeast Louisiana University in 2005. Its comprehensive RefTracker product provides a single interface for all forms of reference (fax, e-mail, phone, in person, and by text) and boasts that webforms, statistics, and a knowledge database of answers can be created without IT intervention.

Mosio/Text-a-Librarian (www.textalibrarian.com)

Mosio, a California-based business-communications company, developed its Text-a-Librarian product specifically for libraries. Available for all major mobile carriers, it offers a secure web-based platform (called a microboard) unique to each library that allows little customization but is very user-friendly. Libraries using this service create a keyword for users to insert at the beginning of their text query. In 2009, it sponsored a "text the American Library Association (ALA)" service for ALA conference attendees who had questions. It provides full technical support and is one of the most inexpensive services for libraries.

UpSide Wireless (www.upsidewireless.com)

Canadian company Upside Wireless claims to have the "widest network coverage" of current telecommunications providers and provides SMS services to corporate clients such as HP, Apple, and Coca Cola. It has tailored its services to individual markets, such as transit systems and libraries, and has promoted the fact that there is no software to download. It uses a Google plug-in that allows library staff to receive the text queries on a Google homepage.

AIM Hack

Before major vendors started pushing their products to libraries, a popular way to employ SMS reference at an institution was to use what is known as the "AIM hack." Kansas State University and Wake Forest University both used this method. ("Libraries Offering" 2010). It employs the same method as other vendors, texting a question to a certain destination number, but uses a work-around in the America Online (AOL) instant messaging system to forward the message onto the library.

MAJOR COMPETITORS

Cha Cha (www.chacha.com)

Calling itself "your mobile BFF," ChaCha is a free service that allows users to text a question 24 hours a day. It launched as a mobile text-for-answer service at the Sundance Film Festival in 2008 and has expanded to provide a voice call-for-answer service. It is increasing rapidly in use, creeping up on Yahoo and Google popularity for "quick searches on the go," according to a June 2009 online *Wired* Magazine article (Singel 2009).

KGB (www.542542.com)

Appearing prominently in television ads in 2009, KGB actually dates back to 1992. It is a fee-based provider of directory assistance and information services. Available 24 hours a day, users can text a question for a fee of $.99 each, in addition to the charges incurred through their mobile provider. Libraries generally do not promote this service because of the cost, but it is an option to know about because of its availability.

A FEW LIBRARIES USING SMS REFERENCE

Southeast Louisiana University library is the first library in the United States to use a reference-by-text-messaging service (Stahr n.d.). Funded by a student technology fee grant in its first year, it launched in 2005. Usage was steady at first, but decreased during Hurricane Katrina later that year. A barrier at first was that, because Altarama was an Australian company, the phone number that users needed to text to was an international number. The library has since updated to a local number. Its library web site (www.selu.edu/library) includes a helpful page describing the service and makes suggestions on what makes a good question for the service.

Curtin University started the first Australian SMS reference service in 2004 (Herman 2007). It used WhileMobile, which converted incoming text messages to e-mails and sent them to reference staff's inboxes. Costs were considered inexpensive to set up (approximately $1,000 USD) and ongoing fees were also inexpensive ($30 per month). Minimal staff training was necessary because all were familiar with e-mail. The library experienced a large number of queries at first, with 200 arriving in a 6-month period. After the initial burst, things slowed to a steady rate with gradual increases, all of which is very manageable by current staff.

The Denton Public Library in Denton, Texas, started using Mosio's Text-a-Librarian service in the spring of 2009. Advertising the service was relatively simple using the company's pre-made publicity fliers and online graphics. Two universities in the area promoted the service to their students as well. Staff training went smoothly; the most difficult thing for staff to remember is to log into the microboard during their reference desk shifts. Librarians report that business is picking up, averaging only one question every few days as compared to one every two weeks in the beginning. However, they resolve to stick with it because all involved see it as a growing trend that is likely to "take off" in the future.

INTERESTING SIDE NOTES

In a November 2000 poll, the Pew Internet & American Life Project asked people who send instant messages online if they have ever used instant messages to "write something that you wouldn't say to somebody's face," and 37% said yes (Simon, Graziano, and Lenhart 2001). Imagine this translating to using SMS messages to ask a question you would not ask to someone's face, and we can layer over it our library's constant battle for patron privacy. Asking a question via SMS, even if the user is in the library 25 feet from a reference desk, allows our patrons a new level of privacy because their query is completely anonymous, with most vendors blocking the actual cell phone number that originated the question.

The limitations to conducting reference via SMS messaging are very apparent. First, there's no real reference interview. The process is intended for short, clear questions with definite answers. There is no room for interpretation or serious research. Speaking of room, a second problem is the limited number of letters in a text message. Librarians, who can become quite excited about the answers to reference questions, must bear in mind that they have 160 characters in which to respond. Sure, you could create a long answer strung out over multiple messages, but bear in mind that your user is paying for each message you send. Another issue is the texting language that users will include in their question. Be sure that reference staff answering SMS reference queries are knowledgeable about the language shortcuts and emoticons used in instant messaging and texting so that they can decipher that "d(^_^)b" means "thumbs up" and ":S" is a sideways representation of "confused."

FUTURE CONSIDERATIONS

The most recent expansion of the SMS reference phenomenon is the idea of collaboration. In July 2009, a group of approximately 50 public and university libraries worked with their SMS vendor, Altarama, to form a consortium of reference responders. Headed by the Alliance Library System in Peoria, Illinois, they promote their project, "My Info Quest," across the country (Hane 2009). This grouping helps to ensure that a query will be answered extremely quickly and perhaps with different perspective. It also expands a library's reference staff—you gain reference librarians from around the country. As with a one-library response center, they are not charging for their answers and have set hours.

Libraries have started to employ tablet computers to promote roaming reference on their public service floors and in the stacks. Perhaps this idea will morph into librarians with smartphones that allow for database and catalog searching, and reference response via SMS.

In the aforementioned Pew "Future of the Internet" report, Josh Quittner of *Fortune Magazine* describes the idea of a "mobile telephone" in the year 2020 as quaint and archaic, a "relic of a bygone era" (Rainie and Anderson 2008). He suggests that telephones will become a communications chip that can be used on any device, like a car key or special wallet. For libraries, this makes little difference; as long as users can still communicate their query to us in one form or another, we will adapt and answer it.

REFERENCES

CTIA—The Wireless Association®. 2009. "CTIA—The Wireless Association® Announces Semi-Annual Wireless Industry Survey Results." Last modified April 1. http://www.ctia.org/media/press/body.cfm/prid/1811.

Hane, Paula J. 2009. "Library Reference Services Are on an Info Quest." *Information Today,* August 3. http://newsbreaks.infotoday.com/Spotlight/Library-Reference-Services-Are-on-an-Info-Quest-55455.asp.

HERMAN, Sonia. 2007. "SMS Reference: Keeping Up with Your Clients." *Electronic Library* 25, no. 4: 401–408.

"Libraries Offering SMS Reference Services." 2010. Library Success: A Best Practices Wiki. Last modified November 15. http://www.libsuccess.org/index.php?title=Libraries_Offering_SMS_Reference_Services.

Rainie, Lee, and Janna Anderson. 2008. "The Future of the Internet III." The Pew Internet and American Life Project, December 14. http://www.pewinternet.org/Reports/2008/The-Future-of-the-Internet-III.aspx.

Simon, Maya, Mike Graziano, and Amanda Lenhart. 2001. "The Internet and Education." The Pew Internet and American Life Project, September 1. http://www.pewinternet.org/Reports/2001/The-Internet-and-Education.aspx.

Singel, Ryan. 2009. "Cool Search Engines That Are Not Google." *Wired Magazine,* June 30. http://www.wired.com/epicenter/2009/06/coolsearchengines.

Stahr, Beth. n. d. "FOCUSED ON: Sims Memorial Library, Southeastern Louisiana University." http://app.info.science.thomsonreuters.biz/e/es.aspx?s=1556&e=8675&elq=df83f6c2f937457b869dd7c5b1c23d53.

Mobile Technologies from a Telecom Perspective

LINDA L. WOODS

AT&T Education Solutions, San Diego, CA 92101

A brief overview of mobile technologies that enable mobile communications and mobile content delivery with an eye to what that means for libraries is discussed.

INTRODUCTION

This article will provide a discussion of technologies that enable mobile communications and mobile content delivery with an eye to what that means for libraries. This article was originally a presentation given at the first annual Handheld Librarian Virtual Conference, July, 2009 (http://www.handheldlibrarian.org).

WHERE WE'VE BEEN

Early Telephone and Telegraph History

1880s – Radio technology began as "wireless telegraphy."
1876 – First telephone invented by Alexander Graham Bell.
1877 – Bell Telephone Company founded.
1885 – Bell began building the nation's original long distance network.
1897 – Marconi wirelessly transmitted signals 3.7 miles.
1890 – Candlestick telephone was used from the early 1890s through the 1920s (Figure 1; Lambert n.d.).

FIGURE 1 Candlestick phone.

1899 – American Telephone and Telegraph (AT&T) became the parent company of the Bell System.

Service Milestones

1915 – First transcontinental telephone line. Service was available to all telephone customers, but at an initial price of $20.70 for the first three minutes between New York and San Francisco.

1919 – First dial telephone system put into service (Figure 2).

1927 – First transatlantic service. Calls traveled across the Atlantic via radio at a cost of $75 for the first three minutes.

1929 – AT&T invented coaxial cable.

1934 – Transpacific telephone service began to Japan. Calls traveled across the Pacific via radio at a cost of $39 for the first three minutes.

Broadband and Mobile Services

1941 – First broadband transmission using coaxial cable.

1946 – AT&T offered mobile telephone service using a single antenna allowing between 12 to 20 simultaneous calls.

1978 – Last manual system converted to dial.

1984 – AT&T divestiture and the break up of AT&T into "Baby Bells."

1983 – Illinois Bell opened the first commercial cellular system in October.

1994 – AT&T acquired McCaw Cellular.

FIGURE 2 Dial telephone circa 1940s.

2000 – Data traffic exceeded voice traffic on the AT&T network.

2005 – SBC bought AT&T and retained AT&T name.

2006 – AT&T purchased Bell South and consolidated Cingular and Yellow Pages (http://www.corp.att.com/attlabs/reputation/timeline/; http://www.corp.att.com/history/milestones.html).

AND THEN CAME CELLULAR TECHNOLOGY

Although mobile services existed in the 1940s, they were rare. Mobile services took a giant leap when AT&T Labs divided wireless communications into a series of cells around 1983. The first cellular services were analog. The second generation of cell phones (2G) are digital.

It is often an overlooked fact that a cell phone is a radio. It transmits cellular, Wi-Fi, global positioning system (GPS), and general packet radio service (GPRS) signals. A cell phone is also a computer. It can translate binary code, deliver content, and authenticate users.

Divestiture in the early 1980s relieved AT&T of its grasp on cellular and broke the company into numerous "Baby Bells." In retrospect, breaking up, shifting around, and recreating itself is nothing new for AT&T (Marshall, Tyson, and Layton 2000).

WHERE WE ARE NOW

3G – It's All About Mobility!

3G simply means third generation. It comprises a suite of communication standards, which include global system for mobile communications (GSM), Edge, universal mobile telecommunications system (UMTS), code division multiple access (CDMA), and worldwide interoperability for microwave access (WiMax). These standards provide the technical specifications for wireless voice, video calls, and data services. 3G allows simultaneous speech and data services, as well as higher data rates. These standards are determined by the International Telecommunication Union (http://www.ity.int/net/home/index.asp).

Short Message System

As a result of the growth and ubiquity of mobile technology, related service components have emerged. short message system (SMS) is a standard that was defined within the GSM standard. It consists of messages of 160 characters. SMS enables services such as Twitter. A common feature is the use of predictive text software that attempts to guess words and increase typing speed. The use of SMS services has led to its own "mini-language" with LOL (laugh out loud) probably the most frequently used.

SMS Examples

Many libraries are experimenting with text reference services. There is a list of libraries using Twitter services at http://www.libsuccess.org/index. php?title=Twitter. Some ways that SMS technology can be used to facilitate library service include:

- Push search results to the patron's mobile phones.
- Notification of materials availability, overdues, or course reading list changes.
- Updates on events, activities, new displays, or new services at the library or on campus.
- Authorize payments/transactions by responding "yes."
- Book drop texts staff that it is full or printer sends message that it needs paper.
- Warn students library is closing or that a group study room is open (geo-messaging pushes message only to users in library).

Lightweight Directory Access Protocol

Lightweight directory access protocol (LDAP) is an Internet protocol that enables access to directory information (such as contacts in an address book) over a network. In addition to searching and reading information, it provides the ability to add, update, and delete information. LDAP can also authenticate users; enforce permissions, and work with a variety of operating systems. It works independently of server, client device, or type of information. Best of all, it is relatively simple and cheap.

LDAP Examples

- Access catalog, see what's available, what's checked out, when it's due back.
- Check course readings that other professors have used in the past or are assigning for current semester.
- Search and download images, audio, video from digital collections.
- Not good for high volume transactional activities, but okay for entries that change infrequently.
- Good for any interface, any operating system, any database, anything that can traverse IP.

Location Based Services

Location based services (LBS) can be used to identify the location of a person or object. There are various types of LBSs. Two of the most common are GPS, which is based on triangulation between the known geographic coordinates of the base stations through which the communication takes place, and GSM, which finds location in relation to cell sites. Other types of LBS include the use of Bluetooth, wireless local area network (WLAN), infrared, and radio-frequency identification (RFID).

LBS Examples

- Pinpoint user's location; then provide directions to buildings and sites; for large libraries, maybe within the building.
- Parcel tracking and vehicle tracking services such as campus shuttle buses.
- Pushing ads or general messages to library patrons when they are within range (Note: Can Spam Act 2005 makes it illegal to send any message to end users without opting in. See http://en.wikipedia.org/wiki/Can_Spam_Act.
- Creating a walking tour or Orientation that "fires" when a participant is within range.
- Tracking the number of users in a specific area could identify bottlenecks or peak usage times. For an interesting example of this, see the MIT SENSEable City Lab project which couples mobile technology with everyday human activity with a view toward urban planning (http://senseable.mit.edu/realtimecopenhagen/).

WHERE WE'RE GOING

A fourth generation (4G) of radio technologies is currently coming into use. It is designed to increase capacity and speed of mobile networks. Called 4G, it is based on 3G. Theoretically, it could allow data transfer rates between

15 and 100 times faster than 3G networks. The main advantages of 4G technology are high throughput, low latency, plug and play, improved end-user experience, simple architecture, lower operating expenditures, and seamless connection to other existing networks.

WHAT IT ALL MEANS

For AT&T

AT&T has extensive experience in the design, deployment, and management of networks and infrastructure. The AT&T network handles 14.5 petabytes of traffic every business day. One petabyte is the equivalent of 100 complete printed collections of the U.S. Library of Congress. As of July 2009, the most traffic ever handled was on September 11, 2001, when there were more than half a billion call attempts.

In terms of the network, in 2009, AT&T spent between $17 and $18 billion to upgrade its 3G network to double the 850 MHz wireless spectrum, expand "backhaul," and increase theoretical peak speed to 7.2 Mbps. (Backhaul is the means by which information is carried from the base station to the central telephone switch.)

For Libraries

There are major changes in the interfaces being used to access information including netbooks, iPhones, smartphones, and other mobile devices. Services are changing to accommodate mobile technologies. In addition, many are just beginning to examine how to provide presence-aware or location-based services.

As the focus shifts from technology and equipment to services, much more traditional activity is taking place "in the cloud," which affects content delivery. One of the most interesting "mash-ups" between information and location is augmented reality. For example, many library patrons find

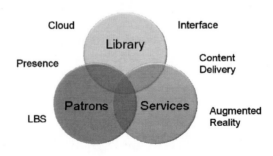

FIGURE 3 Interface diagram.

navigating the library shelves and understanding classification systems confusing. What if there were a way to embed social tags and other information into the stacks in a way that facilitates locating materials? What if the most popular items were featured and suggestions for related materials could be pushed to the user?

It is an exciting time to be involved in mobile technology. Even more amazing is how fast mobile technology is being adopted compared to Internet adoption back in the mid-1990s. Practically every aspect of business, personal life, and academia is changing in ways we could never have imagined 10 years ago. Figure 3 represents some of these changes.

REFERENCES

Brain, Marshall, Jeff Tyson, and Julia Layton. 2000. "How Cell Phones Work." *How Stuff Works*, November 14. Accessed June 10, 2010. http://electronics. howstuffworks.com/cell-phone5.htm.

Lambert, Emily. n.d. "History of the Candlestick Telephone." *eHow.com*. Accessed September 14, 2010. http://www.ehow.com/about_5054538_history-candlestick-telephone.html#ixzz0zZaoZrjq.

Is Mobile Marketing Right for Your Organization?

NANCY DOWD

New Jersey State Library, Trenton, NJ

Is mobile marketing right for libraries? This article investigates that question, using information obtained through the New Jersey State Library's nine Short Messaging Service mobile marketing pilot programs conducted by small, large, urban, county, special, and state libraries.

INTRODUCTION

In 2009, the New Jersey State Library (NJSL) hosted a marketing bootcamp featuring workshops on various marketing techniques. One of the presenters, a representative from Gold Mobile Group, spoke about mobile marketing and described it as an emerging marketing trend that was finding success reaching Hispanic and teen audiences. The NJSL Marketing Department was interested and wondered whether New Jersey libraries would be able to capitalize on this technology.

Beginning May 1, 2009, NJSL partnered with Gold Mobile to create the "mLibraries" pilot program. Ten New Jersey libraries were chosen to test-pilot this new technology to help determine whether mobile marketing was an effective marketing tool for libraries. To get a representation of different types of libraries, NJSL sought libraries representing small stand-alone, large stand-alone, urban, state, special, and system libraries. The following libraries participated in the program: Atlantic County Library

System, Belleville Public Library and Information Center, Burlington County Library System, Cherry Hill Public Library, East Orange Public Library, Johnson Public Library, New Jersey State Library Funding Information Center, New Jersey State Library, Princeton Public Library, and Talking Book and Braille Center. Each library received a free account for one year and was assigned a mobile strategist with Gold Group to develop a marketing plan designed to meet the library's specific goals to reach teens and Gen Y parents. The account provided libraries with an online platform that gave users the ability to use a computer to create exclusive mobile keywords, send and receive text and e-mail messages, and track, report, and archive messages. At the end of the year, each library submitted an evaluative report to the NJSL to be used to help other libraries interested in using this cutting edge technology to promote their services.

Each of the participating libraries in the mLibrary program brought its own particular set of circumstances, needs, and resources to this pilot program. The work of these libraries ultimately helped the NJSL discover how libraries can create an effective mobile marketing campaign.

SHORT MESSAGE SERVICE MARKETING

The Mobile Marketing Association defines mobile marketing as "a set of practices that enables organizations to communicate and engage with their audience in an interactive and relevant manner through any mobile device or network." The tools available include voice mail, texting (short message service [SMS]), mobile search, mobile advertising, social networking, proximity marketing, and apps. Mobile marketing campaigns can be as simple as a voicemail campaign or as sophisticated as the multi-channel election campaign used by President Obama. The valuable feature of a mobile marketing campaign is that it offers the opportunity to have a two-way conversation between organizations and customers.

The NJSL decided to use SMS or texting for the pilot program. Text messaging is a cost-effective, immediate technology that libraries can use to interact with customers regarding vital library information, alerts, special events, and community promotions. Texting has practically become a national pastime. SMS campaigns offer the lowest common denominator because standard cell phone contracts offer unlimited texting for a reasonable cost. Due to the popularity of televisions shows, such as American Idol, that allow viewers to "text in" votes, SMS campaigns are familiar to mainstream America. A texting campaign could provide libraries with the ability to interact with their customers and appeal to the greatest number of people.

The SMS program was affordable and easy to use. There was a minimal start up cost of $100 per library and a monthly fee of $50. Text messages were generated online and anyone with a minimal level of computer skills, a computer, and access to the Internet could work the program.

PROVIDER

The NJSL partnered with Gold Mobile Group for the mLibraries project. Gold Mobile provided guidance at each step of the campaign, helping with marketing strategies and ensuring that the libraries adhered to the legal requirements for mobile campaigns. The company offered a turnkey solution that used an easy-to-use online platform to generate and track messages, provided free training, and assisted in developing marketing strategies.

All of the participating libraries liked the platform and felt the staff was helpful in assisting them and answering questions. Some librarians indicated they were confused about creating polls and, as a result, did not have the type of interactivity they had anticipated.

Gold Mobile had a helpful staff that responded quickly with questions, provided training, and formatted messages before libraries sent them. According to East Orange Public Library's team leaders, Gold Mobile constantly updated our library and gave helpful advice on how to promote the program. They were also very good about helping us with any technical issues we faced when setting up the initial program. Overall, they were friendly and easy to talk to whenever we had concerns.

The Cherry Hill project leader suggested that "It would have be nice if Gold Mobile sent a monthly report to a designated leader—with updates showing the total number of subscribers, how many new for that month, and also how many messages were sent/received." The project leader at Johnson Public Library had a complaint about Gold Mobile's use of military time: "I think it would be more intuitive to just have the time with a.m. and p.m. I definitely sent out a text at three in the morning by mistake!"

TERMINOLOGY

Short Codes and Keywords

Mobile marketing requires participants to use a mobile device to sign up for information. They accomplish this by texting a keyword to a short code or a shortened phone number. There are two types of short codes: dedicated and shared. Dedicated short codes are dedicated to one company and are more expensive than shared short codes. NJSL saved money by using Gold Mobile's shared short codes. Several of their clients had the same short code. Keywords are a collection of letters used to identify a message. These letters can spell out a word but there are never any spaces. Effective keywords are short and easily recognized.

In expensive campaigns (such as American Idol), each contestant had a specific short code and a common keyword. Viewers were told to text "Vote" to their favorite contestant's shortcode. Because the mLibraries program used a shared short code, the keywords played an important role in defining specific campaigns.

LEGALESE

Gold Mobile explained that the mobile industry had applied a strict code of conduct for marketers to prevent abuse. The libraries were given written guidelines. Gold Mobile also offered to review all messages to ensure they were in compliance. The rules were geared toward preventing spam and ensuring it was easy for people to opt out of the campaign. Library staff members who were skeptical about asking people to share their phone numbers welcomed the rules.

Here are six of the most pertinent rules:

1. **Full disclosure is required on all promotional materials**
   People must be informed of certain information in writing on websites, posters, ads, and in the text message. The following are required:

   - Library's identification
   - How many messages the subscriber will receive per week or month
   - The cost to the subscriber. Gold Mobile services are standard rate, meaning there is no charge beyond the carrier's standard charge for texting.
   - How to get help or more information

   This is what the NJSL printed on promotional materials for the New Jersey Library Champions campaign:
   For info about free cool stuff and events, text "CHAMPION" to 5168. Standard message charges apply. Up to 2 messages will be sent per week. To end, text STOP.

2. **The first message must tell people how to get help**
   When a subscriber opts in, an automatic message is generated. Because this is the first message people receive, it needs to include verbiage to let people know how they can get help. The challenge is to convey the message in as few characters as possible. It is helpful to use capital letters and abbreviate when you can. Examples: "Text HELP for help" or "Text HELP for info."

3. **Subscribers must be told how to opt out upon entering the program**
   Signage and text messages need to include verbiage to let people know how they can be removed from a program. Once someone texts STOP, you can no longer send them any messages regarding the program. Examples: "Text STOP to end" or "Text STOP KEYWORD to end" or "To end, text STOP."

4. **Messages must follow formatting guidelines**
   Messages cannot be more then 140 characters long. Character count includes spaces. Paragraph returns count as 2 characters. Certain special

characters, such as accent marks, are not translated properly by the carriers, so make sure to send the message to yourself first so that you can see how they appear on the phone.

5. **Subscribers have rights**

   Mobile marketing works to build the trust of subscribers by establishing rules that will prevent spamming. People opt in from their mobile device. You may only add people from another database when they have subscribed through another opt in process to the same message category. In other words, organizations cannot use exiting mailing lists to add subscribers. The carriers require that you keep a permanent record of all opt ins. Gold Mobile handled all record keeping for the libraries. Subscriber lists cannot be sold or reused for other purposes.

6. **SMS Messaging is not free**

   Text is never considered "free." Even though texting plans have become increasingly affordable, most carriers charge a fee. Thus, the carriers do not permit the word "free" to be used to describe the service. You may, however, use phrases such as "Complimentary service."

THE PILOT PROGRAMS

Seven libraries volunteered to conduct campaigns intended to reach two target audiences: teens and parents of young children. Other target audiences included Spanish-speaking parents of English-speaking children; users of the NJSL's Funding Information; and sports-minded library champions. The overall obstacle for everyone was a resistance to signing up for the programs. The librarians were accustomed to large response rates when they asked people to sign up for e-mail alerts and online newsletters and were very disappointed at getting only one or two people at a time to register to participate in the texting program.

Of the seven libraries that wanted to increase attendance at their teen programs, several libraries sought input about their teens' interests through polls and offered small prizes, such as free movie passes, iTunes, and candy as incentives to participate. Princeton Public Library offered film festival attendees the opportunity to sign up to vote for their favorite film. The Johnson Public Library project leader had the unique problem that teens would show up for programs early and go down the street to the local coffee shop, lose track of time, and miss the programs altogether. She not only wanted to attract new teens to programs, she was also looking for a way to communicate to the wandering teens.

The libraries thought on-the-go parents of young children would appreciate receiving mobile program alerts about upcoming programs and reminders. Overall, the response rate was lower for adults than teens. The team leader for Cherry Hill Public Library found that adults responded better to personal suggestions than promotional materials.

The adult audience is harder to reach through promotional materials only. Most need a word of mouth recommendation or verbal instruction to actually sign up. Although fliers and promotion materials helped raise awareness about the service, verbal instruction at events or hearing about the service from a friend reached more adults and was more affective in gaining the adult subscriber.

The East Orange Public Library (EOPL) developed a campaign to reach Spanish-speaking parents of English-speaking children. The libraries offered many programs for children but because of the language barrier Spanish-speaking parents were unsure whether programs were free or even if their children were allowed to participate and were afraid to bring their children. With four librarians on staff who were fluent in Spanish, the EOPL created a campaign that invited parents to receive text alerts about upcoming programs and other free children's services in their native language. Post cards, which included photos of the four librarians, were printed in Spanish. The campaign was met with resistance from parents who were afraid they might be charged or were distrustful of giving out their phone number. The idea of using this technology to reach people in their native language is an excellent idea but would need to be part of a larger campaign that included outreach and relationship building through community leaders and organizations to be effective.

The State Library conducted two pilots. One focused on creating a relationship with users of the NJSL's Funding Information Center (FIC) and to drive them to seek additional information on a newly formed blog. The other served as one of many communication channels in a statewide campaign intended to recruit sports enthusiasts to sign up for the NJ Library Champions program.

The FIC project had an uphill battle because the project leader was trying to promote a new service with a new medium to a small group of users. She suggested the program may have been a better fit for their Mid-Day Training sessions.

> The training sessions have started filling up quickly and waiting lists can get long, so I think some attendees would have preferred receiving texts when new registration forms became available. The texts would have been an easy way to send reminders about upcoming classes instead of relying on email. I could have also done surveys or sent texts with relevant information after class.

The NJ Library Champions SMS project posted four billboards along heavily trafficked roadways featuring famous NJ Library Champions: New York Yankees pitcher A.J. Burnett, New Jersey Devils hockey player Zach Parisi,

Philadelphia Eagles football player Trent Cole, and New York Giants football player Justin Tuck. Although only 144 people responded, the names provided the library with a targeted database of names. That list was used to communicate news, special events, and promotions about the NJ Library Champions program. The NJSL project leader was pleased with the initial results of the campaign and could envision future uses.

> We believe one value of the SMS program is that it can connect libraries with people who are on-the-go and who might not already be library users. We can imagine using this program to engage people at shopping centers, sports and entertainment venues. The key, of course, is to make sure you are offering something valuable to your audience.

Two county libraries participated in the pilot. Atlantic County Library (ACL) has ten branches with a central marketing department that runs its campaigns. Burlington County Library (BCL) has seven branches, each is responsible for its own marketing.

Both systems had identified parents of young children and teens as the audiences they wanted to reach and both felt it was best to run branch-based campaigns rather than system-wide. "We felt there was more interest in information specific to each branch rather than information about the system as a whole. We did try some messages that went to everyone, usually about services such as databases," commented the ACL project leader.

OBSTACLES

All of the libraries experienced sign-up resistance. Suggested causes included inadequate phone plans and lack of staff buy-in. Many people were apathetic and did not see it as a benefit. The project leader for Bellville Public Library, a small urban library in northern New Jersey, said her teens were more comfortable with social networks than mobile.

> The teens were very resistant to join because the majority of them do not have unlimited texting, so they do not want to use up their valuable text messages. Also, they were concerned that parents would not let them, or that they would get in trouble. Most told me that they would rather use MySpace or Facebook. The teens who did join were concerned with the number of texts they would receive. I made a deal that I would send one text a week, at the very most. They were not interested in contests or games via text, probably because of the fact that they do not have unlimited texting.

The Burlington County Library Team Leader cited several issues his libraries faced. There were a range of factors that came into play, ranging from people with no cell phone or no text message plans to people who get too many text messages and did not want another source of noise. The leader explained, "Personally, I think one of the major issues was staff buy-in. Training of staff was never an issue, but keeping people going on the project was always a concern."

BEST PRACTICES

Use All Communication Channels

The original premise for the pilot program was that libraries should identify one or two target audiences and create campaign-specific promotional materials encouraging people to subscribe. The NJSL provided bookmarks, poster templates, and large stand-up banners to the libraries. The strategy that ended up working best was to integrate the campaign into all the communication channels the libraries offered. Cherry Hill Public Library had great success by adding the mobile call-to-action on all library media, banners, posters, bookmarks, newspaper calendar event listings, and websites.

Best Practices: Communication Channels

Be sure to identify the following on all promotional materials and website listings:

- The intended target audience—who will benefit by the program
- The call to action—what is the keyword and short code people have to enter
- What they will get—what kind of information and how many messages
- Why it's great—why is it valuable to people
- Regulation compliance—the legalese including how many messages people will get, the cost, and how to opt out of the program

Keywords

Keywords are the letters people text to opt in for a program. Some of the libraries experimented with a different keyword for each specific program. Others chose one keyword for the teen audience and one for the adult audience. The Cherry Hill teen team leader explained it this way:

> For our teens we chose to use the keyword "NOISE," because this is the name of our monthly teen events calendar as well as our blog: *Noise Online*. Consistency is definitely key when trying to build a "brand" or marketing yourselves as we are trying to do with the term "NOISE." I think it was a good choice in that the teens didn't have to remember

anything new, we were just simply adding a service to a "brand" we had already started to establish.

The system allowed libraries to track the number of responses for each message and keyword. That feature made it easy to test different words to determine whether one was more successful than another. Keywords were also used to create responses for polls and surveys.

Best Practices: Keywords

- Create a special keyword for each event so you can track responses
- Use your imagination to create "catchy" words
- Keywords should be short and easy to remember
- Don't mix letters and numbers
- Pick a keyword that makes sense to your target audience

Staff Training and Participation

As with any new program, it is important to offer staff training. Gold Mobile provided training for staff members responsible for creating and sending messages, but it was up to each library to train the staff on customer service techniques. Although many staff members were uncomfortable with the concept of texting, some were already actively texting and offered little resistance. Mobile marketing is a highly personal mode of communication and people need to have a good reason to opt in. Therefore, it is essential to help staff understand and communicate the benefits to the customer. Because many customers might not know how to opt in, it is important to train staff how to help people register on their phones. The most successful libraries were able get buy in from staff members, especially those who had direct contact with customers. Cherry Hill's team leader suggested that an instructional video showing people how to opt in (with a person going through the steps) posted on the Library's web site and Facebook page would be helpful for both staff and customers.

Best Practices: Staff Training and Participation

- Share scenarios with staff of how the texting program can benefit customers.
- Create bookmarks that staff can easily share with customers.
- Train staff to mention the programs and offer to demonstrate how to sign up.
- Ask for staff volunteers to act as mentors for other staff members.

- Encourage staff to opt in to text programs to familiarize themselves with the experience.
- Experiment using the programs for internal operations: work schedule change notifications, holidays, staff events, etc.
- Post news items about successful campaigns other companies are conducting.
- Post positive feedback from customers in the staff room.
- Keep staff informed of all campaigns.

Engaging Program Participants

Mobile marketing allows libraries to reach people directly through the one device they use throughout the day—their cell phone. Always keep in mind that customers will not opt in unless they are confident the information they will be getting is worthwhile. The major advantage of the SMS program for a library is that it can provide a two-way communication channel with customers through the use of polls and surveys. Librarians can use this feedback to tweak existing programs or create new programs that will enhance future experiences.

Best Practices: Engaging Program Participants

- Parents of young children can vote for the next story time book, suggest programming, and provide feedback about existing programs through SMS polls and surveys.
- Book Fair attendees can sign up to receive scheduled and special reminders of events throughout the day.
- Customers interested in specific topics can sign up to receive notification that additional guidance and information are available, such as online brochures, pertinent programs, or new resources.
- Computer class attendees can register, collect input, receive reminders, vote for next topics, and provide feedback.
- Book club members can sign up to receive new arrival alerts, discussion topics, and meeting reminders.
- Job seekers can sign up to receive alerts on upcoming job fairs, resume writing workshops, and job seeking tips.

CONCLUSION

Of the ten libraries in the pilot program, four have indicated they would want to continue using mobile marketing. Those who declined the service felt that not enough people participated in the program to justify spending

$50 a month. Two libraries would like to continue with Gold Mobile. The Talking Book and Braille Center will be partnering with NJSL to explore ways to use mobile marketing as part of the library's fundraising efforts. Johnson Public Library staff liked the service but will use Yahoo's free texting service that allows users to send SMS messages to anyone on their contact list. Staff will remind teen volunteers of the dates that they have signed up for via text this summer. The team leader explained, "I am going to use Yahoo to send out the texts because it is free and I will know exactly who I am sending the texts out to."

The teen leader at Cherry Hill Public Library would like to continue the service with Gold Mobile and offered this recommendation:

> I would suggest mobile marketing to other libraries. It was extremely affordable and helpful in staying connected to the teens and to demonstrate that we are up-to-date with what's going on in technology today. It also made it easier to stay in contact with teens that you're not able to see every day in order to let them know what events are going on.

The NJSL learned that although mobile marketing can produce targeted databases and a platform to create two-way communication with people, libraries must provide a compelling reason for people to agree to participate. Libraries that have existing marketing strategies in place and that are genuinely looking for customer input achieved the greatest success.

APPENDIX: PARTICIPATING LIBRARIES

Atlantic County Library System (10 branches)
Project Leader: Karen George
Team Members: Mary Beth Fine, Branch teen librarians
Belleville Public Library and Information Center
Project Leader: Karyn Gost
Burlington County Library System (7 branches)
Project Leader: Andy Woodworth
Team Members: Joan Divor, Dawn Ferris, Judy Howard, and Adam Crockett
Cherry Hill Public Library
Adult Project Leader: Katie Hardesty
Teen Project Leader: Michelle Yeager
Team Members: Robyn Bland and Meghan MacLauchlan,
East Orange Public Library
Project Leader: Nathalia Bermudez and Carla Segarra
Team Members: Christal Blue and Emily Crowel
Johnson Public Library, Hackensack
Project Leader: Keri Adams

New Jersey State Library
Funding Information Center Project Leader: Andrea Simzak
Library Champions Program Project Leader: Nancy Dowd
Team Member: Gary Cooper
Princeton Public Library
Project Leader: Tim Quinn
Team Members: Janie Hermann and Susan Conlon
Talking Book and Braille Center
Project Leader: Elizabeth Burns

Handheld E-Book Readers and Scholarship: Report and Reader Survey

NINA GIELEN

ACLS Humanities E-Book, American Council of Learned Societies,
New York, NY

This is an executive summary of ACLS Humanities E-Book's white paper Handheld E-Book Readers and Scholarship: Report and Reader Survey, *which details the results of findings on the use of digital scholarly monographs for research purposes on various handheld reading devices. The white paper also includes an overview of the process of converting titles for handheld e-readers, including costs.*

EXECUTIVE SUMMARY

This report describes a conversion experiment and subsequent reader survey conducted by ACLS Humanities E-Book (HEB) in late 2009 and early 2010 to assess the viability of using scholarly monographs with handheld e-readers. Scholarly content generally involves extensive networking and cross-referencing between individual works through various channels, including bibliographical citation and subsequent analysis and discussion. Through past experience with its online collection, HEB had already determined that a web-based platform lends itself well to presenting this type of material but was interested in exploring which key elements would need to be replicated in the handheld edition to maintain the same level of functionality, as well as what specific factors from either print or digital publishing would have to be taken into account. As sample content, HEB selected six titles from its own online collection (three in a page-image format with existing OCR-derived text and three encoded as XML files) and had these converted by an outside vendor with minimal editorial intervention into both MOBI (prc) and ePub files.

During its in-house assessment phase, HEB experienced some navigational difficulty with both formats and found that annotation and other interaction with the text was difficult using several popular e-readers. (Specifically, the sample titles were tested by HEB on the Sony Reader PRS-700, Amazon's Kindle 2, and the Stanza application on the Apple iPhone.) HEB also found the XML titles to be of limited functionality in the MOBI format, and therefore opted not to further poll readers on this subset.

Approximately 88% of our 142 survey participants expressed overall satisfaction with the appearance and functionality of the three remaining handheld samples, although roughly half reported some level of frustration with the search function using either format, and only 26% felt they would have an easy time citing and referencing these editions. Satisfaction with other interactive features, such as adding notes, bookmarking and highlighting, was noticeably higher; however, the "n/a" (not applicable) option was also selected frequently for these categories, and it appears that a large number of participants were unable to perform the tasks in question due to confusing or insufficient instructions from the device manufacturer. As formats evolve, future satisfaction with these features may increase. Irrespective of specific limitations, 75% of participants were interested in potentially downloading additional similar titles for free or if priced below $10.

HEB's production costs, starting from preexisting OCR-derived text and XML files, amounted to approximately $204 per title for creating both editions: ePub and MOBI. As an example for other publishers, were we to process 300 additional titles from our online collection, this cost would increase to approximately $232 (for a bulk conversion of page-image titles only, which are somewhat more expensive to convert than XML). Therefore, if titles were sold at $10, production costs would be offset at 24 downloads. This data is included to provide publishers with a basic idea of conversion costs from one digital format to another; however, it does not take into account other ordinary overhead charges or management fees and discounts for third-party retailers and distributors, which would need to be factored in separately.

HEB's initial findings in this study indicate that titles formatted for existing handheld devices are not yet adequate for scholarly use in terms of replicating either the benefits of online collections—cross-searchability, archiving, multifarious interactive components—nor certain aspects of print editions that users reported missing, such as being able to mark up and rapidly skim text. A turnaround is underway once a common and more robust format optimized for handheld readers is determined and devices themselves evolve, adding improved display options and better and more intuitive web-access, searching, and other interactive use of content.

To read the full text of the study, go to: http://www.humanitiesebook. org/heb-whitepaper-3.html.

The E-Book Lifestyle: An Academic Library Perspective

JULIE SHEN

California State Polytechnic University, Pomona, Pomona, CA

This case study describes an academic library's experiences in managing e-book collections amidst escalating expectations from users. A survey of student habits and attitudes reveals a steadily growing readiness to access e-books via handheld devices. Faculty use of e-books is also increasing. Current developments in the mobile technology market are addressed alongside issues of content, format, and marketing.

INTRODUCTION

Over the past several years, we have seen extraordinary momentum building toward wide adoption of e-books by the general public. According to the Association of American Publishers, e-book sales experienced a 118.9% increase in the first half of 2010 compared to the same period in 2009 (Jordan 2010). Online retailer Amazon.com reported even more dramatic increases: a 300% increase in sales of its Kindle e-books in the first half of 2010 compared to the first half of 2009 (Amazon.com 2010). Among Kindle rivals, the Sony Reader store had more than 10 million e-books downloaded by users in May 2009 alone (Sony Corporation 2010), and Barnes and Noble, maker of the Nook reader, reportedly captured 20% of the e-book market in less than a year (Barnes and Noble 2010).

Many public libraries have responded to rapidly changing user expectations by offering downloadable e-books. Currently, approximately 5,400 public libraries offer downloadable e-books through vendors such as Overdrive and NetLibrary (Rich 2009). By comparison, the move towards downloadable e-books has practically been non-existent in academic libraries.

E-BOOKS: THE LAST 10 YEARS

A decade ago, it could be said that the reverse was true. This was a time when many academic libraries started making e-books available to their users, California State Polytechnic University, Pomona (Cal Poly Pomona) included (Dowdy, Parente, and Vesper 2001; Snowhill 2001). As part of the California State University (CSU) system, which has 23 campuses throughout California, its e-book collection management began in the CSU Chancellor's office, and some of it still takes place centrally. Within this system, each campus library has significant autonomy, and Cal Poly Pomona has adopted numerous e-book packages on its own. A small but significant part of its e-book collection is e-reference, and over the past five years in particular this part of the reference collection has increased while the print collection has become much smaller in size. In addition to the e-book packages and e-reference, subject librarians also select e-books on a title-by-title basis. However, the vast majority of its titles still come from e-book packages.

In 2008, more than 800 of Cal Poly Pomona students participated in an annual survey conducted by the EDUCAUSE Center for Applied Research that examined undergraduate students and their use of technology. Students were asked about their use of laptops and library services. According to the survey results, more than 80% of students owned a laptop. As a result, they were able to make use of the Cal Poly Pomona wireless network from anywhere on campus. Also, approximately 98% of our students had high-speed internet at home, and an astounding 85% of students visited the Cal Poly Pomona library's web site once or more per quarter.

It is therefore unsurprising that although our print circulation has been on the decline since 2003–2004 (Figure 1), our e-book usage has been increasing since 2005 (Figure 2). Although Levine-Clark (2007) observed that print books are still preferred over e-books in the humanities, we have not observed this differentiation; student use of our humanities e-book collection has been increasing steadily since 2006–2007 (Figure 3).

WHITHER HANDHELD?

According to the 2010 Horizon Report, published by the New Media Consortium, mobile computing is expected to become mainstream on

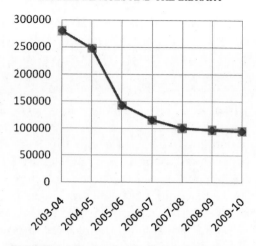

FIGURE 1 Print books checkout and renewals.

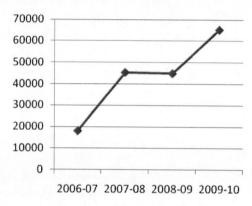

FIGURE 2 ACLS, NetLibrary, and safari e-Books (all users, monthly average, on- and off-campus).

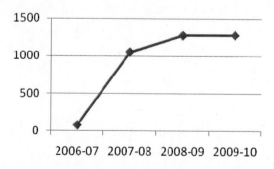

FIGURE 3 Student use of ACLS Humanities E-Books (monthly average, off-campus only).

college campuses within the year, and e-books will follow suit in two to three years (Johnson et al. 2010). Mobile computing refers to handheld devices, the general categories being smartphones and personal digital assistants (PDAs), with specific examples being the iPhone, iPod Touch,

Palm, or any number of Android phones. Handheld devices also include slightly larger devices such as subnotebooks and tablet PCs, the best known being the Apple iPad. In this case, "e-books" is shorthand for e-book readers, such as the Amazon Kindle, the Sony Reader, and more recently, the Barnes and Noble Nook.

Approximately five years ago, Cal Poly Pomona considered piloting an e-book reader project using the Amazon Kindle but decided the device was too fragile for mass lending. The Kindle and the Sony Reader have since been the subjects of several experiments by academic libraries, which have lent them to users with great success (Figure 4). There is little doubt that an e-book reader project would have been popular at Cal Poly Pomona. According to the EDUCAUSE Center for Applied Research study, approximately 11% of our students considered themselves "innovators" in terms of technology adoption, and 29.5% were "early adopters" (Rogers 1983). This was higher than students overall, who rated themselves at 9.5% and 25.9%, respectively (Table 1).

In the same survey, students were also asked about their use of smartphones. More than 67% of Cal Poly Pomona students owned an "Internet-enabled phone," and roughly half of these students took advantage of this feature.

THE CASE OF THE MISSING PROFESSOR

An important question to consider for academic librarians is whether faculty are also reading e-books. According to Schonfeld and Housewright's (2010) survey of faculty habits and attitudes, only 50% of faculty believed in the

- Cal Poly San Luis Obispo

  http://lib.calpoly.edu/learningcommons/services/checkouts/
  kindle/

- Duke http://library.duke.edu/ereaders/

- Fairleigh Dickinson University

  http://view.fdu.edu/default.aspx?id=7467

- Penn State

  http://libraries.psu.edu/psul/lls/sony_reader.html

- Texas A & M http://library.tamu.edu/services/media-
  reserves/borrow-a-kindle

FIGURE 4 E-book reader programs at academic libraries.

TABLE 1 2008 ECAR Study of Undergraduate Students and Information Technology

	Cal Poly Pomona (800)	All students (26,000)
I love new technologies and am among the first to experiment with and use them.	10.9%	9.5%
I like new technologies and use them before most people I know.	29.5%	25.9%
I usually use new technologies when most people I know do.	44.9%	51.4%
I am usually one of the last people I know to use new technologies.	10.1%	9.3%
I am skeptical of new technologies and use them only when I have to.	4.5%	3.9%

importance of preserving e-books, and less than half of these faculty deemed e-books important for teaching or research. In rating the importance of a variety of electronic resources for teaching and research, e-books came in last place, below "free, web-based education resources" (p. 23). A faculty committee at Stanford University predicted that it will be at least another 50 years before faculty will replace print with e-books (C-LIB 2008).

A recent study by the National Endowment for the Arts could shed some light on the seemingly radical difference between faculty and student attitudes. Titled "Reading on the Rise," the optimistic report showed the sharp reversal of a 25-year decline (National Endowment for the Arts 2009). Adults who read literature (in print or online) increased from 46.7% in 2002 to 50% in 2008. A large number of people read e-books, a habit reported by more than 20% of adults ages 18 to 34 and by less than 15% of adults ages 45 to 54. The difference is equally pronounced when looking at reading of other types of e-texts (articles, blogs, or essays), a habit reported by more than 50% of adults ages 18 to 34 and only 40% of adults ages 45 to 54. In light of these results, the difference between faculty and students would seemingly reflect a generational divide.

At Cal Poly Pomona, this difference can be observed in e-book usage statistics. Although faculty use of e-books has increased steadily since 2006 (Figure 5), this increase is occurring much more slowly compared to student usage (Figure 6). Over a period of four years, off-campus faculty use of e-books almost doubled, whereas student use more than tripled.

NEXT STEPS

Currently, e-book reader programs at academic libraries have all been limited to pleasure reading. This is a reflection of the relative wealth of fiction titles available for e-book readers. A significant number of general non-fiction titles are also available for these devices. However, the selection

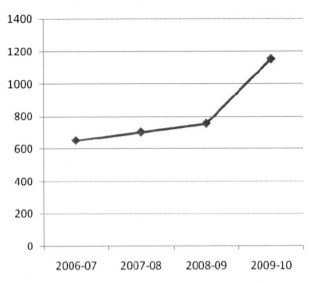

FIGURE 5 Faculty use of E-Books (monthly average, off campus only).

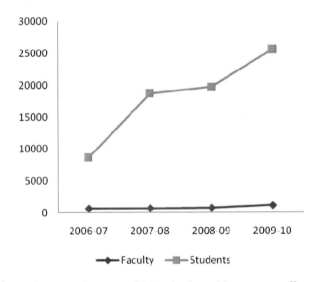

FIGURE 6 Faculty vs. student use of E-Books (monthly average, off campus only).

of academic titles seems paltry by comparison. Another issue is that these projects have all been device-dependent. Because users naturally gravitate toward a wide variety of devices, academic libraries that want to make handheld e-books available to faculty and students should make device independence a priority. In this arena, the health sciences have had a head start. Smartphone adoption among physicians has reached an all-time high at 94%, and an impressive variety of medical reference titles are available for download to these devices (Logan and Collins 2009; Shereff 2010; Spyglass Consulting 2010). Many health science libraries are accustomed to making downloadable e-books available to future doctors, a good example being the University of Iowa Libraries (http://guides.lib.uiowa.edu/pdas).

Regarding content and format, the American Council of Learned Societies (ACLS) recently conducted an e-book experiment that should give pause to academic libraries and publishers alike (Gielen 2010). In this experiment, ACLS made three of its titles available in two different formats suitable for handheld devices: MOBI and EPUB. A total of 142 respondents downloaded a title onto an e-book reader, such as a Kindle or a Sony Reader. More than 90% reported high satisfaction with the reading experience. Users varied in their satisfaction with various features related to academic use, such as the ability to bookmark (87% satisfaction), highlight (68% satisfaction), and make notes (53% satisfaction). An astounding 75% indicated an interest in downloading future academic titles, with many indicating a desire to do so at a lower price and some specifically requesting access through their library.

Perhaps the most important consideration regarding e-books for academic librarians is marketing. Students who would be happy to use e-books often did not realize such titles were available through their university libraries (Jenkins 2008; Lonsdale and Armstrong 2010). A quick search on the community portal at LibGuides.com reveals that some libraries are trying to fill this gap by creating research guides that point their students to hidden e-book collections, but more work needs to be done in this area.

The most startling addition to the handheld discussion may be the claim that having a downloadable format does not really matter (Croft and Davis 2010). Certainly, recent changes in mobile technology have pointed in this direction. For example, a recent usability test showed that, although most e-books in Cal Poly Pomona's current collection were next to unreadable on smaller mobile devices such as the iPod Touch, all of our titles worked well on larger mobile devices such as the Apple iPad. With Dell, Samsung, and Blackberry maker RIM all slated to release tablet PCs to compete with the iPad and wireless Internet access's increasing availability across the United States (http://wigle.net; boosting faculty and student awareness of our current e-book collections and their anytime, anywhere features just might render moot the downloadable e-books debate for academic libraries (Gallagher 2010).

REFERENCES

Amazon.com. 2010. "Amazon.com Now Selling More Kindle Books than Hardcover Books." Last modified July 19. Accessed September 16, 2010. http://phx. corporate-ir.net/phoenix.zhtml?c=176060&p=irol-newsArticle&ID=1449176.

Barnes and Noble. 2010. "2010 Annual Report." Accessed September 16, 2010. http://www.barnesandnobleinc.com/for_investors/annual_reports/annual_ reports.html.

C-LIB Subcommittee on Digital Information Technologies in the Research Library Environment at Stanford. 2008. "Report of the C-LIB Subcommittee on Digital Information Technologies in the Research Library Environment at Stanford." Accessed September 16, 2010. http://facultysenate.stanford.edu/2008_2009/reports/SenD6153_c_lib_dig_info.pdf. Palo Alto, CA: Stanford University.

Dowdy, Jackie, Sharon Parente, and Virginia Vesper. 2001. "Ebooks in the Academic Library." Sixth Annual Mid-South Instructional Technology Conference, Murfreesboro, Tennessee, April 8–10. Accessed September 16, 2010. http://frank.mtsu.edu/~itconf/proceed01/21.pdf.

Gallagher, Dan. 2010. "Is RIM Making the Right Move with a Tablet?" *Marketwatch.com*, September 24. Accessed September 24, 2010. http://www.marketwatch.com/story/research-in-motion-has-a-tough-sell-on-tablets-2010-09-23.

Gielen, Nina. 2010. "Handheld E-Book Readers and Scholarship: Report and Reader Survey." ACLS Humanities E-Book White Paper No. 3. Accessed September 16, 2010. http://www.humanitiesebook.org/heb-whitepaper-3.html.

Johnson, Laurence, Alan Levine, Rachel Smith, and Sonja Stone. 2010. "The 2010 Horizon Report." Accessed May 31, 2010. http://wp.nmc.org/horizon2010/.

Jordan, Tina. 2010. "AAP Reports 10.6% Increase in June Book Sales: E-book Sales Up 204.2% for the Year to Date." The Association of American Publishers. Last modified August 19. Accessed September 16, 2010. http://www.publishers.org/main/PressCenter/Archicves/2010_August/June2010Statistics.htm.

Logan, Penny, and Seana Collins. 2009. "PDA Survey of Medical Residents: E-books Before E-mail." *Journal of the Canadian Health Libraries Association* 30: 3–10.

Lonsdale, Ray, and Chris Armstrong. 2010. "Promoting Your E-books: Lessons from the UK JISC National e-Book Observatory." *Program: Electronic Library and Information Systems* 44: 185–206.

National Endowment for the Arts. 2009. "Reading on the Rise: A New Chapter in American Literacy." Accessed September 16, 2010. http://www.nea.gov/research/Research_brochures.php.

Rich, Motoko. 2009. "Libraries and Readers Wander into Digital Lending." *New York Times*, October 14. Accessed September 16, 2010. http://www.nytimes.com/2009/10/15/books/15libraries.html.

Rogers, Everett. 1983. *Diffusion of Innovations*. New York: Free Press.

Salaway, Gail, and Judith Caruso. 2008. "The ECAR Study of Undergraduate Students and Information Technology, 2008." Accessed May 31, 2010. http://www.educause.edu/ECAR/TheECARStudyofUndergraduateStu/163283. Boulder, CO: EDUCAUSE Center for Applied Research.

Schonfeld, Roger, and Ross Housewright. 2010. "Faculty Survey 2009: Key Strategic Insights for Libraries, Publishers, and Societies." ITHAKA S+R. Accessed September 17, 2010. http://www.ithaka.org/ithaka-s-r/research/faculty-surveys-2000-2009/faculty-survey-2009.

Shereff, Denise. 2010. "Electronic Books for Biomedical Information." *Journal of Electronic Resources in Medical Libraries* 7: 115–25. doi: 10.1080/15424065.2010.482903

Snowhill, Lucia. 2001. "E-books and Their Future in Academic Libraries." *D-Lib Magazine* 7 (7/8). Accessed September 16, 2010. http://www.dlib.org/dlib/july01/snowhill/07snowhill.html.

Sony Corporation. 2010. "Annual Report 2010." Accessed September 16, 2010. http://www.sony.net/SonyInfo/IR/financial/ar/2010/index.html.

Spyglass Consulting. 2010. "Study: Physicial Smartphone Adoption Experiencing Exponential Growth." Last modified July 23. Accessed September 23, 2010. http://www.spyglass-consulting.com/press_releases/SpyglassPR_POC_Comm_Physicians_2010.v1.0.pdf.

University of Iowa. 2010. "PDA and Smartphone Resources." Last modified September 1. Accessed September 16, 2010. http://guides.lib.uiowa.edu/pdas.

EBSCO*host Mobile*

RON BURNS

EBSCO Publishing, Ipswich, MA

SARA ROFOFSKY MARCUS

Queensborough Community College, Bayside, NY

The explosive growth in mobile technology coupled with widespread adoption among students, librarians, medical professionals, and corporate users means that research database providers need to be where the users are. EBSCOhost Mobile was designed and developed to provide EBSCOhost database users with a platform that makes the power of EBSCOhost and its content highly accessible on the most popular smartphones and mobile devices.

INTRODUCTION

EBSCO Publishing (EBSCO) is the world's premier database aggregator, offering a suite of more than 300 full-text and secondary research databases. Through a library of tens of thousands of full-text journals, magazines, books, monographs, reports, and various other publication types from renowned publishers, EBSCO serves the content needs of all researchers (academic, medical, K-12, public library, corporate, and government). The company's product lines include proprietary databases such as *Academic Search, Business Source, CINAHL, DynaMed, Literary Reference Center, MasterFILE, NoveList, SocINDEX,* and *SPORTDiscus*, as well as dozens of leading licensed databases such as *ATLA Religion Database, EconLit, INSPEC, MEDLINE, MLA International Bibliography, The Philosopher's Index,*

PsycARTICLES, and *PsycINFO.* Databases are powered by EBSCO*host,* the most-used for-fee electronic resource in libraries around the world.[1]

With the EBSCO*host* platform, EBSCO develops technologies, interfaces, and access tools for all types of users: young, old, computer novices, advanced searchers, librarians, non-English speakers, users with physical disabilities, doctors, nurses, business researchers, historians, DIY'ers, application developers, computer users, and now even mobile device users. More people have advanced mobile devices now; Gartner reported that more than 40 million smartphone units were sold in quarter two of 2009 and another 41 million in quarter three of 2009.[2] Improvements in mobile technology have brought a new level of sophistication to what users are able to do with smartphones and other Internet-enabled mobile phones. Handheld devices have moved beyond phone calls, and users expect a lot of functionality from their equipment.

Interesting mobile statistics abound. Techcrunch exposed that 65 million members reach Facebook via mobile devices every month, or 26% of the 250 million total active members.[3] Nielsen in its Top Mobile Sites/Brands for 2009 lists companies such as Yahoo and CNN (i.e., search and content web sites) as the most used on mobile Internet enabled devices.[4] These facts were even more of an indication that EBSCO*host* could prove to be a successful mobile solution for libraries. In ReadWriteWeb's *Mobile Web's Explosive Growth,* the iPhone was the top smartphone worldwide with "traffic to prove it"; "Android is rising fast" and "smartphones are taking over as mobile web grows."[5] This data helped the EBSCO technology team's understanding of the most popular platforms to prioritize support when building and testing a mobile solution.

Prior to 2009, EBSCO had experience with mobile platforms. A text-only interface that was developed approximately 10 years ago served dual purposes as an accessible interface (at the time, text-only interface options were a standard solution for accessibility) and a more readable alternative for personal digital assistant (PDA)/mobile users because it had no images and little JavaScript. With EBSCO*host*'s accessibility redesign in 2008 and the launch of EBSCO*host Mobile,* EBSCO has since retired the text-only interface. In 2005, *DynaMed*, EBSCO's evidence-based medical product, was ported to Palm and Windows Mobile native applications. The *DynaMed* end user audience was the driving factor for this move because primary care medical professionals were the earliest adopters of PDA/mobile applications. Other driving factors were the necessity of offline portable access for bedside use and for doctors working in developing countries that have weak Internet infrastructure (e.g., Africa and Haiti, where EBSCO regularly donates subscriptions). *DynaMed* also highlighted a common mobile development dilemma—when does it make sense to build a native mobile application versus a mobile web site application?

EBSCO*HOST MOBILE* WALKTHROUGH

The explosive growth in mobile technology coupled with widespread adoption among students, librarians, medical professionals, and corporate users means that research database providers need to be where the users are. In December 2009, EBSCO released EBSCO*host* Mobile, allowing researchers to access their EBSCO*host* databases via smartphones and other handheld devices.

EBSCO*host Mobile* was designed for usability on small devices and in particular was optimized for smartphones (iPhone, BlackBerry, and Treo), the most common handheld devices with Internet browsers. Smartphones as a target platform were an early development and testing consideration, excluding support for Wireless Application Protocol (WAP) devices and making JavaScript a requirement. Prioritization was still a challenge. EBSCO, like other mobile vendors, had to grapple with the "death matrix" of infinite Device/Operating System (OS)/Network provider combinations. To this day, the mobile browser market lacks standardization and is very fractured. Testing was focused on the most popular devices and operating systems with a quality certification process for the most popular smartphones at the time, including iPhone, BlackBerry, Dell Axim (Windows Mobile OS), Palm 750 (Palm OS), and Android OS. A beta period solicited customer feedback on many others, knowing from the start that testing all combinations of Device/OS/network providers was impractical. Many mobile developers choose only to focus on Webkit browser platforms for the biggest bang-for-buck (i.e., you get Apple's Safari and Android), but we knew EBSCO had to go further.

The application was focused on the core searching and viewing functions of EBSCO*host*. The interface was designed for a lower resolution and simplified by removing folders and other more advanced features for increased speed and user convenience. All databases currently available on the EBSCO*host* platform are available via EBSCO*host Mobile* and can be searched together in multi-database search.

The focus of the home EBSCO*host Mobile* screen is a simple search box. In addition, it offers other options, such as choosing which EBSCO*host* database(s) to search, setting search options, accessing field codes, and specifying preferences. Many of the existing EBSCO*host* features such as search modes, limiting to full-text, date ranges, peer-reviewed content, or by publication name are available. Users can also search images on the Mobile interface.

The result list is scrollable and available data includes citations, *Image Quick View,* access to full text articles, and an e-mail results function. Clicking into a result replicates the EBSCO*host* user experience, providing researchers with information including author information/affiliation, links to the source, document type, subject terms, NAICS/Industry codes along with the abstract, ISSN, Accession Number, persistent links, images, links to full text, HTML, PDF (some devices require a PDF reader plugin), and e-mail as the primary delivery tool.

Some favorite EBSCO*host* features didn't make sense on Mobile (such as printing) and were omitted. More features may be added later if smartphone browser technology improves and customer requests dictate.

In addition to providing access to smartphone users, EBSCO*host Mobile* will open up access to research databases for many who need computer access in remote regions that may have slow or unreliable Internet access because it uses only a fraction of the bytes per page compared to regular EBSCO*host*. Some examples already in use include: rural public libraries, international locations, corporations with researchers in remote locations using satellite links, and cruise ships.

With the new *EBSCO Discovery Service,* libraries can enable mobile access to their library catalogs. Catalog records display with book jackets and metadata, as well as direct links to the Online Public Access Catalog (OPAC).

Two frequently asked questions are "How do I log into EBSCO*host Mobile?*" and "What is the direct URL to use for my EBSCO*host Mobile* profile?" If a user is not authenticating through an institution's proxy, another form of authentication is required, such as an EBSCO user ID and password or a library card number. A new shortened URL was set up for mobile users (m.ebscohost.com) as well. Depending on how an institution's administrator has configured its authentication types, the direct login to the EBSCO*host Mobile* profile may look like the following link: http://search. ebscohost.com/login.aspx?authtype=ip,uid&profile=mobsmart. The EBSCO Support site also has FAQs available.

Getting started requires some administration, but it's a simple setup process within EBSCO*admin*. A profile is created that can contain a specific list of databases and library customizations, which involves only three steps: add databases, choose the authentication method, and add the link to your library web site. Many authentication methods are available to choose from, as with EBSCO*host* where proxy is still the most popular and can be integrated into most existing proxy login processes. This separate profile requirement also allows libraries to access specific usage reports and statistics on their patron mobile access.

FUTURE ENHANCEMENTS AND IPHONE APPS

Some of the future enhancements on the roadmap include auto-detection of mobile devices offering a toggle between personal computer/desktop versions, a warning for non-qualified devices accessing to set expectation for possible cosmetic display issues, the capability for libraries to brand and skin the interface, mobile formatted PDFs for certain products (e.g., *Business Book Summaries*), and native iPhone applications. With release expected in Fall 2010, EBSCO*host* for iPhone/iPod Touch/iPad will allow the same EBSCO*host Mobile* experience with additional features, including the ability to save content locally for offline viewing and landscape viewing options.

LIBRARY PROMOTION

Academic and public library promotion ideas are plentiful on the Web; there are several examples of what other sites have done to let patrons know about mobile access to EBSCO*host*. Sites can promote EBSCO*host Mobile* as a platform, a specific database solution (e.g., *CINAHL* Mobile), or a patron blog topic. Sites may also use EBSCO*host Mobile* as a library's entry into the mobile Internet. For those still skeptical about investing in mobile platforms and their short-term promise in the library, sites can dip a toe in without any extra financial investment by offering EBSCO*host Mobile* as an extended library service to patrons. Posters and other promotional materials are also available at ebscohost.com to help sites promote the service and all sites are encouraged to take advantage of these resources.

SETTING UP EBSCO*HOST MOBILE* AT YOUR LIBRARY: ONE LIBRARY'S EXPERIENCE

Both the Electronic Resources/Web Librarian and an MLS candidate at an urban public 2-year community college that is part of a multi-campus university system shared trials and successes they faced while setting up mobile access to the EBSCO*host* databases in 2009. This library utilizes a proxy server, EzProxy, for off-campus authentication, and IP authentication for on-campus access to all library electronic resources, including databases provided by EBSCO*host*. The two presenters shared not only their experiences, trials, tribulations, and triumphs, but also those of their colleagues in the university system as the presenters' campus was among the first to adopt and implement the EBSCO*host Mobile* interface.

The first issue considered was the Digital Divide. This was also one of the biggest concerns. The presenters tried to figure out how to support those patrons and colleagues who love technology and are among the early adopters of any new technology, while not forgetting those patrons and colleagues who are reluctant and late adopters of any technology due to fear, lack of knowledge, or other reasons. The presenters also needed to consider the Digital Divide in terms of access—the hardware and Internet access.

The next issue to be considered was how to provide librarians, staff, and technical support for the hardware students are using to access EBSCO*host*

Mobile. The broad range of mobile devices available makes supporting each device virtually impossible. The sheer number of devices makes it improbable for any library staff to maintain proficiency in their use.

Another issue was usability of the devices for those unaccustomed to the small screen and keypad or touchscreen for keyboard access. The screen itself is very similar to that of the traditional EBSCO*host* interface. However, the ability to offer research support was limited because the research screen was very different in terms of size and viewability. For those patrons on their own devices, there was also the issue of Internet access (i.e., dataplans or wireless network access costs). Patrons need to be made aware of these costs before accessing the EBSCO*host Mobile* interface to perform research.

At the presenters' library, authentication to use the wireless network was via a login screen that is not optimized for mobile devices. This made the need to access the network itself an issue separate from accessing EBSCO*host Mobile.* For those accessing EBSCO*host Mobile* via their own dataplan, there would be the issue of EzProxy authentication, again not always optimized for the mobile device's smaller screen.

For any mobile interface, there is an inherent need for a mobile device, or hardware. EBSCO*host Mobile*, by its very nature, would seem implicitly to require special hardware. It was discovered that special hardware was needed only to use EBSCO*host Mobile* as it was originally intendedL as a method to access the EBSCOhost databases from a mobile device.

EBSCO*host Mobile*, as implied by its name, seemed to require a mobile device capable of accessing the Internet. Many patrons at the library in question have one or more of these devices already. If the patrons are already comfortably using these devices, perhaps we as librarians can interest them in doing research using their own devices.

A serendipitous use of the EBSCO*host Mobile* interface was found to be on traditional computers with slow Internet connections. The interface loaded faster and required less bandwidth than the traditional EBSCO*host* interface. This benefit shrinks the Digital Divide because materials previously inaccessible due to slowness and timeouts now became accessible. However, a problem with this was the lack of printing features on the interface, requiring the patron to e-mail or download the article for later printing.

Participants in the session were asked about what works for them and their future plans for promoting EBSCO*host Mobile.* Of those who currently had EBSCO*host Mobile* available, more than half noted they used the library's homepage to advertise, whereas approximately one-third used posters and less than 10% used public service announcements. None of the participants had used informative handouts. An issue with how these methods have worked in the past is the length of the URL and how to make the URL easiest to use for the patrons.

Participants were also asked about other successes they had in using and promoting EBSCO*host Mobile*. Among those mentioned were demonstrations and presentations in library classes, either by having the students use their own devices or the librarian passing around a device; workshops led for faculty at other participants; institutions; e-mail blasts with URLs that work (such as with URL shorteners); word-of-mouth advertising; Quick Response (QR) code on posters or publications; flyers with tear-offs containing the URL; and the library newsletter. Participants also indicated posting the access code in online courses. This would only work if students were accessing the course through their own device.

Participants were also asked about their future promotion of the EBSCO*host Mobile* interface. More than half noted that they would use the library's homepage, approximately 5% would use informative handouts, approximately 10% would use posters, and approximately one-quarter would use public service announcements.

The EBSCO*host Mobile* interface not only broadens the range of access through additional devices, but also enhances usability for those on slower Internet connections or with older computers. Advertising and promoting the EBSCO*host Mobile* interface needs to address both of these issues.

NOTES

1. EBSCO Publishing, http://www.ebscohost.com (accessed January 19, 2010).

2. "Gartner Says Worldwide Mobile Phone Sales Declined 6 Per Cent and Smartphones Grew 27 Per Cent in Second Quarter of 2009," Gartner, August 12, 2009, accessed October 5, 2009, http://www.gartner.com/it/page.jsp?id=1126812.

3. Erick Schonfeld, "About a Quarter of Facebook Users Connect Via Mobile Phones," *TechCrunch*, September 3, 2009, accessed October 5, 2009, http://www.techcrunch.com/2009/09/03/about-a-quarter-of-facebook-users-connectvia-mobile-phones.

4. "Top Mobile Phones, Sites and Brands for 2009," *NielsenWire*, December 21, 2009, accessed January 19, 2010, http://blog.nielsen.com/nielsenwire/online_mobile/top-mobile-phones-sites-and-brands-for-2009/.

5. Sara Perez, "Mobile Web's Explosive Growth," *ReadWriteWeb*, October 29, 2009, accessed December 15, 2009, http://www.readwriteweb.com/archives/admob_reports_on_mobile_webs_explosive_growth.php.

Index